ADVENTURES IN FUGAWILAND

A COMPUTER SIMULATION IN ARCHAEOLOGY

Third Edition

T. Douglas Price and Anne Birgitte Gebauer

University of Wisconsin–Madison

Computer Program by Peder Gebauer

Original Program by T. Douglas Price and Michael J. Kolb

Mc Graw Hill

Boston   Burr Ridge, IL   Dubuque, IA   Madison, WI   New York
San Francisco   St. Louis   Bangkok   Bogotá   Caracas   Kuala Lumpur
Lisbon   London   Madrid   Mexico City   Milan   Montreal   New Delhi
Santiago   Seoul   Singapore   Sydney   Taipei   Toronto

McGraw-Hill Higher Education *∽*

A Division of The **McGraw-Hill** *Companies*

4 5 6 7 8 9 0 VFM/VFM 0 9 8 7 6 5 4

Library of Congress Cataloging-in-Publication Data

Price, T. Douglas
    Adventures in Fugawiland : a computer simulation in archaeology / T. Douglas Price and Anne Birgitte Gebauer.—3rd ed.
      p. cm.
    Includes index.
    ISBN 0-7674-2724-6
    1. Archaeology—Computer simulation. I. Gebauer, Anne Birgitte II. Title.
CC175.P75 2001
930.1'0285'5369—dc21   2001054612

Sponsoring editor, Phil Butcher; *production editor,* Jennifer Mills; *manuscript editor,* Margaret Moore; *design manager and cover designer,* Violeta Diaz; *art editor,* Emma Ghiselli; *production supervisor,* Pam Augspurger. This text was set in 11.5/14 Garamond Book by TBH Typecast, Inc., and printed on 45# Scholarly Matte by Von Hoffmann Graphics.

www.mhhe.com

For Jennifer, Erika, and Annalise

PREFACE

Adventures in Fugawiland first appeared in 1988 and has provided an in-class experience with archaeological fieldwork to thousands of under-graduate and graduate students since then. One reason for its success and longevity is that *Fugawiland* focuses attention on the nature of archaeological data and its interpretation. Students have to deal with information they have obtained from excavation and determine how this data reflects what people actually did in the past.

Fieldwork is the most stimulating intellectual activity that archaeologists undertake. Physical labor, long hours, and the ambiguous, hard-to-grasp nature of archaeological data force one to think deeply about the meaning of the information that is sought. Fieldwork can also be one of the most enjoyable activities that archaeologists pursue. Working with a like-minded group of individuals in the search for the buried history of past peoples is a fascinating process.

Many people, however, never have the time or opportunity to partici-pate in archaeological fieldwork. *Fugawiland* provides some of that experience without the investment of the time, travel, expense, and energy that fieldwork requires. *Fugawiland* is intended to help you understand the kinds of information that archaeologists obtain from fieldwork and how to interpret what it may mean.

The third edition of *Fugawiland* has been substantially revised and upgraded. Part 2 has been expanded, particularly Chapter 1, "The Dis-covery of Archaeological Sites." The section on contour maps has been expanded to clarify how these maps are drawn. Chapter 3, "Analysis and Interpretation," has been elaborated with some corrections in the sec-tion on radiocarbon dating and more discussion of technology, social organization, and ideology. Further refinements and corrections have been included in the remaining chapters to improve the overall experi-ence with *Fugawiland*.

The major changes in *Adventures in Fugawiland* for the third edition are in the computer portion of the exercise. The computer program (by Peder Gebauer) has been completely rewritten in C+ to make it faster and more amenable to the number of photographs that have been added. *Fugawiland* now comes on a CD, which allows us to include more information. We have added a substantial color component in the form of photographs of archaeological fieldwork that we hope will add to the flavor of the experience. Some of the multiple-choice questions have been improved, and the overall program has been enhanced.

Many of these corrections, additions, and improvements have been suggested by the readers and reviewers of *Adventures in Fugawiland.* We would particularly like to thank Ronald Lippi of the University of Wisconsin Colleges, Curtis Hoffman of Bridgewater State College, and Scott Paffenroth, Lance T. Biechele, and others who provided helpful suggestions. In addition, the teaching assistants in our course in introductory archaeology at the University of Wisconsin–Madison have been a constant source of information for revisions and corrections. Those individuals include Brad Chase, Kildo Choi, Lane Fargher, Caroline Funk, Jonathan Haws, David Meiggs, and Nicole Misarti. Thanks are also due to the reviewers of the manuscript who have helped us further improve this edition, including Laura Junker, Western Michigan University; Priscilla Schulte, University of Alaska Southeast; Jim Skibo, Illinois State University; and John Staeck, College of DuPage. Finally, it is essential to thank our former editor, Jan Beatty, and the staff of Mayfield/McGraw-Hill, including Jen Mills, Violeta Diaz, and Emma Ghiselli, who have helped us put together the volume now before you. We hope you will enjoy and learn from *Adventures in Fugawiland.*

CONTENTS

Hardware Requirements and Installation Instructions

Adventures in Fugawiland, Third Edition, is intended for use with Windows operating systems. Hardware requirements and installation instructions are provided below. Macintosh users should obtain *Adventures in Fugawiland,* Second Edition, Macintosh version.

HARDWARE REQUIREMENTS

CPU 80386 or newer, 2MB RAM, VGA monitor with at least 256 colors, CD drive. Windows 95, 98, NT 4.0, Me, 2000, or XP.

INSTALLATION INSTRUCTIONS

Installation automatically begins when you insert the CD. If the CD auto play feature is disabled on your computer, go to "My Computer," double-click on the CD icon, and then double-click "Setup."

HELP

If you are having problems with *Fugawiland* and your computer, there are several sources for assistance. First, contact your instructor or advisor at your computer center. Second, if you are still experiencing a problem, contact McGraw-Hill Technical Support at (800) 331-5094 or techsup@mcgraw-hill.com. Third, if your problem is still not resolved, please contact Peder Gebauer at netpxg@netscape.net.

PART 1

AN INTRODUCTION

You are about to embark on an expedition of archaeological discovery. Most archaeological materials lie beneath the ground, invisible to the naked eye, and are very expensive and time consuming to uncover. A computer, however, can simulate both the archaeological data and what archaeologists actually do—things that are difficult to grasp just from reading textbooks or scientific articles.

FUGAWILAND

Fugawiland is a computer program that will give you an idea of what it is like to excavate prehistoric sites and to study archaeological information. Maps and drawings produced by the computer offer new views of archaeological data. Fugawiland should provide you with a sense of how archaeological sites appear on the landscape, what aspects of the environment may be important to human existence, what basic archaeological information looks like, how archaeologists think about their data, and what problems they face.

The Program

This workbook is intended to lead you through Fugawiland. The computer program is largely self-explanatory and "user-friendly," but successful understanding of the project and completion of the assignment require some time with this workbook. The workbook is a kind of field guide and notebook that you should follow and fill in as you go along. You might also use a word processor along with Fugawiland to keep some notes and to write up your final interpretation of the site.

The Workbook

Use this workbook as a log of your activities, both in the Report section in Part 4 and throughout the book. Use the margins and blank pages to

Workbook Sections

A typical excavation scene.

record notes, sketches, and any other information you may need. When you have completed the assignment, both in the workbook and in the computer program, turn in the printed answer sheet from the computer along with Part 4 from this workbook to your instructor.

This workbook has several parts. Part 2, "Doing Archaeology," discusses general archaeological concepts and methods archaeologists use to discover and excavate sites. Part 3, "Using the Computer Program," briefly describes the Fugawiland computer program and explains how to use it. Part 4, "Report of Investigations," is the section in which you conduct your studies and write a report of investigations about Fugawiland. This is the section you will turn in to your instructor. Part 5, "For Further Study," lists other books on archaeology and related topics, as well as information on opportunities for actual archaeological fieldwork. There are a glossary of key terms and an index at the back of the workbook. These sections are described in more detail below.

DOING ARCHAEOLOGY

Part 2, "Doing Archaeology," is the field manual and covers some of the methods and concepts of archaeology. This part includes Chapters 1, 2, and 3. Chapter 1, "The Discovery of Archaeological Sites," describes how archaeological sites are found and explains some aspects of archaeological survey. Chapter 2, "Archaeological Excavation," discusses the methods of archaeological excavation and how archaeologists obtain information about the past. Chapter 3, "Analysis and Interpretation," describes how archaeologists examine the materials recovered in excavations and how they develop an understanding of the past. Some of the more important terms and concepts used in archaeology are discussed in Part 2.

It is important to note here that archaeology is not a "do-it-yourself" activity. Most professional archaeologists have advanced degrees and have spent a great deal of time in the field and in the classroom learning the many facets of the discipline. Trading in antiquities or disturbing archaeological sites without permission is illegal in most states and punishable by fines and/or imprisonment. Archaeological materials are valuable cultural resources and part of our inheritance from the past. It is essential that everyone understands this and works toward their care and curation.

USING THE COMPUTER PROGRAM

Part 3, "Using The Computer Program," exposes you to prehistoric archaeology through a computer simulation of a variety of artifacts, a series of archaeological sites, and a large study area—a hierarchy of archaeological information. This section of the workbook takes you through the computer simulation and provides additional information about archaeological investigations. Part 3 includes Chapters 4-8.

Chapter 4, "The Menus," introduces the simulation and gives an overview of what to expect. Use this chapter as a guide for your travels through Fugawiland. Chapter 5, "Regional Map of Fugawiland," and Chapter 6, "Excavating Sites," provide you with more information about specific aspects of research in Fugawiland, including finding sites, excavating, and analyzing the data from such studies. Chapter 7, "Site Plans," provides access to the drawings and contents of the sites you excavate. Chapter 8, "Analysis of Data," gives some instructions and ideas about how to look at the information you have collected in the excavations. This is the heart of Fugawiland, where you investigate the archaeological information you have collected.

REPORT OF INVESTIGATIONS

Part 4, "Report of Investigations," is the section in which you conduct analyses and summarize the results of your study of Fugawiland and the prehistoric human groups that lived there. This section is a summary of your thoughts and impressions of Fugawiland. Here, you will describe how the people lived, their technology, what they ate, seasonal changes

in their lives, and their beliefs. Be sure to fill in all the required information, drawings, and the like as you create your report. The multiple-choice questions in the computer program are an objective way of evaluating what you learned about Fugawiland.

FOR FURTHER STUDY

Part 5, "For Further Study," contains more information about archaeology and Fugawiland, including a list of books and articles on archaeological concepts and fieldwork, method, and theory, that may be of interest if you want to know more about the subjects discussed in this workbook. This section also lists some information on opportunities for archaeological fieldwork.

Other Features

There are several features in the workbook intended to make your job easier. Technical words are highlighted in **boldface** in the text and defined in the glossary. Turn there for more information on new terms and concepts. Boldface is also used to indicate specific instructions you need to follow as part of the assignment. Paragraph headings in the margins give you an outline of the text and make it easier to locate specific information. Finally, numerous drawings, photographs, and other illustrations give you a better visual impression of the information that is being presented.

The Fugawiland project is intended to be both educational and fun, so grab your electronic shovel and begin your adventure in Fugawiland!

Good luck!

PART 2
DOING ARCHAEOLOGY

CHAPTER 1

THE DISCOVERY OF ARCHAEOLOGICAL SITES

Archaeology is the study of the human past, from the time of our earliest ancestors, some 5 million years ago, to the present. The basic information archaeologists use to learn about the past comes from artifacts and sites. **Artifacts** are the objects and materials that people have made and used. **Sites** are accumulations of such artifacts, representing the places where people lived or carried out certain activities. Much of the information gathering for archaeological studies requires **fieldwork** to discover artifacts and sites.

Archaeology

METHODS OF ARCHAEOLOGICAL INQUIRY

Artifacts and sites are found either on the surface or beneath the ground. **Surveys** are used to discover artifacts on the ground, **testing** is done to learn if buried materials are present, and **excavations** are used to expose buried materials. These are the primary discovery techniques of field archaeology. This chapter tells you about archaeological survey and how prehistoric sites are discovered. The next chapter focuses on the techniques of archaeological testing and excavation.

Fieldwork

One way to think about the problem of discovering archaeological sites is to consider a hypothetical or imaginary area like Fugawiland. To understand the past in a place like Fugawiland, archaeologists must locate the places where people lived and left the remains of residence and other activities. Finding sites requires a combination of methods that includes both library research and fieldwork.

Fugawiland

The discovery of archaeological sites depends in part on what is already known about an area in terms of its landscape, environment, and history. Prior to beginning fieldwork, archaeologists check the relevant

Archival Research

An air photograph of an effigy mound in southern Wisconsin, approximately 800 years old. The mound has been outlined in white.

written material on the time period and place of interest. This research will reveal the present state of knowledge, indicate what is not known as well as what is, and help establish directions for further research. Such library research is also essential to ensure that investigations similar to the ones you are planning have not already been done.

The next step is a visit to the local historical society or other archaeological institutions such as museums or university departments, where records of the area are maintained. These institutions generally keep an archive of information on the location and contents of known archaeological and historical sites. Study of these archives will indicate what types of sites are already known and perhaps their size and general content of artifacts. This information can provide an initial list of sites in the area and their locations on maps.

Maps

Maps are one of the most important tools of fieldwork. **Topographic maps** (showing the **topography,** or shape, of the land surface with contour or elevation lines) are available for most areas. In the United States, the U.S. Geological Survey compiles and distributes these maps. These topographic maps are the standard means of recording geographic location. Such maps contain a great deal of information about longitude and latitude, elevation, slope, and the location of water, roads, towns, and other features. This information is essential to understand the location of the site on the landscape with respect to water, strategic routes, and other resources.

Air Photos

Air photographs can also provide information on the location of archaeological sites. Old foundations or prehistoric agricultural fields,

overgrown with vegetation and almost hidden on the surface, may appear in air photographs. When prehistoric structures were originally abandoned, the depressions often filled with rich topsoil, which means better growth conditions for vegetation. In wheat fields, for example, such different soil conditions might result in a distinctive pattern showing the outlines of houses or whole villages. Such patterns are best observed from low-flying planes during a dry period in the early summer.

The next step in discovering the past involves fieldwork. An archaeological survey is a systematic search of the landscape for artifacts and sites. It is not always possible to make a complete survey of the entire area under investigation. Roads, forests and other vegetation, and construction often cover substantial parts of the landscape. It may be possible to thoroughly survey only a portion of the entire area, but that portion, known as a **sample,** should be representative of the larger region under investigation. (More information on sampling appears on page 73.) The larger the proportion of the research area that can be surveyed the better.

As a start, all landowners in the selected area should be contacted to learn what they have found previously on their lands, to examine any collections of artifacts they may have, and to obtain permission to survey their property.

Archaeological field survey involves systematic field walking. This means walking up and down cultivated fields and exposed surfaces. The intervals between the paths are determined by the size of the sites that may be in the area. For example, if the smallest sites are likely to be

Field Walking

Surface survey and collecting artifacts. The flags mark places where tools were found.

20 m in diameter, there is a good chance of finding them by walking at intervals of 10–15 m. It may also be necessary to walk over an area several times during the year, or over several years, to collect enough artifacts to determine the contents and approximate age of a site.

Recording Information

When an artifact is found, the location of the find is recorded and the object is put in a bag. The surrounding area should be searched carefully by walking back and forth at close intervals. It is important to determine whether the artifact is a single isolated find or whether there are more artifacts or unusual discolorations on the surface that might indicate features like fireplaces or pits. If there is a site, it is important to establish the area covered by artifacts to determine the size of the site and to obtain an estimate of the density of artifacts.

Information must be recorded about each find spot. These **field notes** should include (1) the location, site number, map number, which field, and location on the field such as distance or compass orientation to characteristic nearby features in the landscape; (2) what was found, types and number of artifacts, fire-cracked stones, charcoal, and so on; and (3) site observations such as discoloration in the soil that might indicate cultural layers or pits, the presence of mounds, nearby streams or water, and other pertinent environmental information.

A description of the conditions for making observations might also be useful information for later comparison of what was found at different places. A newly plowed field where stones and potsherds have been

exposed by a recent rain offers the optimal conditions for surveying. Dusty conditions, vegetation, stony ground, or dim light make observation much more difficult.

CONTOUR MAPS

Information from the field survey can be plotted on a map to provide a better record of the location and distribution of the finds. A **contour map** shows the topography, the three-dimensional surface of the place. One way to visualize a contour map is to look at a three-dimensional map of a high hill or mountain as in the first drawing on page 12. In this case the mountain has two peaks with a saddle, or low area, in between. The contour lines on this 3-D depiction reveal the shape of the mountain. The view of this mountain from directly above would appear as a two-dimensional contour map.

Another way to think about contour maps is shown in the second drawing on page 12. The top image is a side view of a volcanic island. Elevations of the island between sea level (0) and 3700 feet are marked by horizontal lines at 500 ft. intervals. If the lines were marked on the

Mapping the Site

Chapter 1 The Discovery of Archaeological Sites **11**

A contour or three-dimensional map of a hill with two peaks.

(a) Volcanic island with contour lines drawn around it at the same elevation at 500-ft intervals. (b) The contour lines on the island seen from directly above it produce a contour map. (Adapted from Doug Latimer, Rocky Mountain Hiking.)

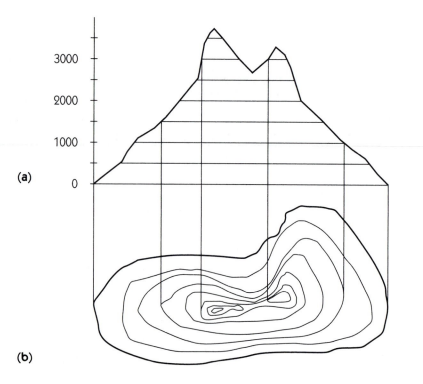

(a)

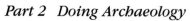

(b)

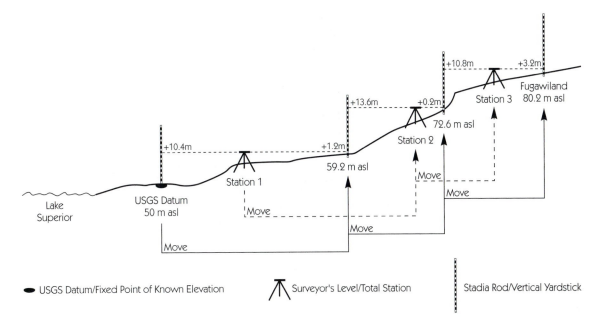

+10.8m   +3.2m
+13.6m   +0.2m   Fugawiland
                    80.2 m asl
+10.4m   +1.2m   Station 3
                    Station 2
          72.6 m asl
          59.2 m asl
Station 1
Lake   USGS Datum
Superior   50 m asl

Move   Move   Move   Move

● USGS Datum/Fixed Point of Known Elevation   ⋀ Surveyor's Level/Total Station   ▌ Stadia Rod/Vertical Yardstick

Measuring elevation from one point to another by moving surveying instrument and stadia rod.

white volcanic ash with dark soil and viewed from directly above, the island would look like a contour map (the bottom image).

The elevation of the ground is measured in feet or meters above sea level or some other fixed point of known elevation, called a **datum.** The United States Geological Survey (USGS) has placed these fixed points all over the country so that surveyors can measure from them and establish the elevation, latitude, and longitude of a place. Surveyors use an instrument known as a **level, alidade,** or **transit,** to determine the elevation from the fixed point to the new area. Modern surveyor's instruments, known as **total stations,** use lasers and computers to quickly and accurately measure both distance and elevation.

The drawing above shows how to measure from a fixed datum to a new area and determine the elevation there. The measurement begins at a datum placed by the USGS at an elevation of 50 meters above sea level (asl). The level is first set up at Station 1 some distance away and aimed at the USGS datum. A measuring stick (stadia rod) is placed on the datum, and the height of the level instrument above the datum is measured. In this case the instrument is 10.4 m above the datum. The stadia rod is then moved inland some distance to a higher elevation and the level turned to read the elevation of this new location. Now the level, which has not moved, reads 1.2 m. That means that the ground where the stadia rod stands is 9.2 m (10.4 − 1.2) higher than the USGS datum, or 59.2 m asl.

Next, the level is moved to Station 2 past the stadia rod that is kept in place. Reading the stadia rod from the level at Station 2 results in a height of 13.6 m. Now the level is at an elevation of 73 m (59.4 + 13.6).

A site is found. Intensive surface collections are made in order to pick up artifacts that may help date the site. One archaeologist holds a stadia rod to measure the elevation.

The stadia rod is then leapfrogged past Station 2 to higher ground. The new reading on the stadia rod is 0.2 meter above sea level. The ground under the stadia rod at this point is 0.2 m below the height of the level, or 72.8 m asl. Next, the surveying instrument is leapfrogged to Station 3 and aimed back at the stadia rod at 72.8 m for a reading of 10.8 m. Then the stadia rod is moved to the edge of Fugawiland and measured from the level at Station 3 to be 3.2 m. From those measurements, we calculate the elevation at the edge of Fugwiland to be 79.8 m asl. The accompanying table shows the measurements and calculations for this example.

	DATUM	STADIA	LEVEL	STADIA	GROUND
Station 1	50 m	+10.4	60.4	-1.2	59.2
Station 2	(59.2)	+13.6	72.8	-0.2	72.6
Station 3	(72.6)	+10.8	83.4	-3.2	80.2
Fugawiland	80.2				

From this point we can measure the elevation of the topography of Fugawiland in terms of meters above sea level. To produce a contour map, a grid is laid out across Fugawiland and measurements of the elevation of the ground are taken at regular intervals across the grid. A contour map is a series of concentric contour lines at different elevations in the area. An example is shown below. Elevation, or contour, lines are drawn on the map connecting points of equal elevation. Concentric contour lines are normally drawn at a regular interval, for example, 1 meter or 500 feet. In the example, the interval is 10 meters.

It is necessary to interpolate values between measured points when drawing lines in order to plot the specific contour. This can be done by actually measuring on the map or simply estimating the value between the two points. For example, in the example, values between 99 and 103 m and between 95 and 103 m are shown as measured to determine where the 100-m contour line crosses between the measured grid points. The result in its simplest form looks something like the edges of a wedding cake seen from above. Each line provides an outline of the shape of the landscape at regular intervals of elevation. Lines that are close together indicate a steep slope; widely spaced contour lines indicate a flat area or gentle slope.

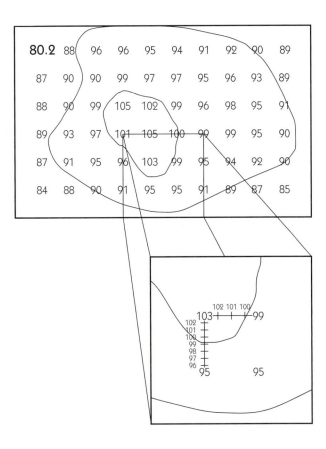

The exploded square shows how values are interpolated to produce a contour map.

A contour map is made by recording the measurements of elevation taken across the site and their locations on the site grid. Contour lines are then drawn by connecting points with similar elevations. A kind of level known as an alidade sits on the drawing table.

Another way to visualize a contour map is to imagine horizontal planes through the landscape, as shown on page 17. Each plane runs through a specific elevation such as 5, 10, and 15 m above sea level. Seen from above these planes describe a series of irregular circles around the higher features of the landscape—the higher the features, the more contour lines needed to describe it. The land above the contour line is higher than the line, and the land below is lower.

The contour map, then, is simply the outlines of all the contours of the landscape projected onto the flat surface of a map. Contour maps are also used to show the topography of other kinds of information. In the Fugawiland project, you will be asked to draw contour maps of elevation, phosphate levels, and artifact counts.

BURIED SITES

Archaeological remains are often buried in the ground beneath the sediments that have accumulated since their deposition. Objects found on the surface often have been brought up from deeper layers by digging or plowing. Materials found on the surface usually provide only a partial indication of the information that can be obtained from a buried site.

Coring and Test Pits

Once buried sites have been located, surveyed, and mapped, other kinds of fieldwork can reveal more about them. Drilling or boring into the ground with an auger or corer produces a column of soil showing the

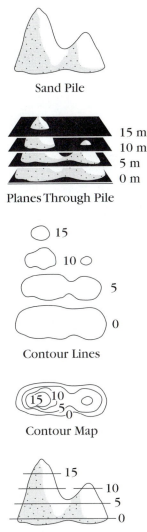

Sand Pile

Planes Through Pile

Contour Lines

Contour Map

Sand Pile

Source: Adapted from D. Greenwood, Mapping *(Chicago: University of Chicago Press, 1944), p. 78.*

sequence of layers and samples of sediments at the site. Small **test pits,** perhaps a square meter in size, dug into the ground can provide similar information and might be necessary to determine if a buried site is present. A number of corings and/or test pits often are made at regular intervals over the surface of the site. Soil samples should be collected from all parts of the site and at different depths.

Physical and chemical analysis of soil samples may provide information about the origins of the deposits, the water content and fertility of the soil, the amount of organic material, and the basic chemistry of the soil. **Phosphate analysis** of the sediments from a site may reveal traces of human activities. Phosphate is found in bone, feces, urine, and other organic matters that accumulate in and around human habitation. When

Soil Analysis

A 1-square-meter test pit.

hydrochloric and ascorbic acid are added to a soil sample, phosphate shows up as a blue color. Areas with higher concentrations of phosphate will show up as stronger blue colors in such analyses.

Phosphate testing may supplement surface surveys in areas where vegetation prevents observations of the surface or where cultural layers are deeply buried beneath the topsoil. Within a known habitation area, these tests may be used to determine the extent of the site and detect special areas such as house floors.

Soil Contents

Other objects in the soil are also informative. Materials found in soil samples often include pieces of wood and plants, seeds, fragments of insects, mollusk shells, hair, and chips of bone or stone. Such items provide information on the formation of the layers, the local environment, and the nature of past human activities. For example, small chips that result from the manufacture of arrowheads and other stone tools can come up in borings and test pits, indicating that other buried artifacts may be present.

Geophysical prospecting is used to detect disturbances in the subsoil and the presence of prehistoric features and disturbances. These methods include measurements of magnetic variations in the ground and of the electrical conductivity (resistivity) of the soil and the use of ground-penetrating radar.

Prospecting Methods

Metal detectors register the presence of metal objects both lying on the surface and buried in the soil. Metal detectors emit an electromagnetic field that is disrupted by the presence of metal objects in the ground. Metal detectors are of limited value because they do not detect nonmetallic objects and most archaeological sites in North America do not contain metals.

Metal Detectors

Variation in the composition and water content of different soils results in differences in electrical conductivity. The use of a **resistivity meter** to measure soil conductivity can provide a map of soil differences, which may be related to the presence of prehistoric disturbances such as fireplaces, house foundations, and burial sites.

Soil Resistivity

Ground-penetrating radar is a new technique for studying archaeological sites. Electromagnetic waves in the form of **georadar** are sent into the ground, something like the sonar used in submarine hunts. Low-energy radar waves register anomalies or disturbances in the subsoil, which are shown on a graph. Such anomalies may be caused by nature

Georadar

or by human activities. Excavation is usually required to identify such disturbances.

A FINAL NOTE

Prehistoric sites are often found through a combination of archival research and fieldwork. Archival research provides information on what is already known about an area. Fieldwork often results in the discovery of the unknown. When new sites are discovered, surface survey, testing, boring, and several geophysical methods are available to determine the size and possible contents of the prehistoric deposits. However, once a site is discovered and defined from the surface, excavations are often necessary to expose what lies underground.

CHAPTER 2

ARCHAEOLOGICAL EXCAVATION

Excavation is the technique that archaeologists use to uncover buried remains from the past. Buried materials usually are more abundant and better preserved than those found on the surface. In excavations, accurate information can be observed on the arrangement and relationships of structures, artifacts, plant and animal remains, and other materials. Thus, excavation often is essential to obtain more information about the past.

Excavation

A large excavation is assisted by an excavating machine.

Excavations are conducted to answer specific questions that the archaeologist would like to resolve. Who lived at the site? What did they eat? What were their daily activities? Where did they get raw materials for making tools and equipment? What kinds of relations did they have with their neighbors? How was their society organized and structured? Learning the answers to such questions is one of the reasons most archaeologists got interested in the subject in the first place.

THE EXCAVATION DIRECTOR

Directing an excavation requires a variety of skills and knowledge. The director must plan the field season, raise money to pay for the work, supervise and train a crew of volunteers or students, record the information from the site with drawings and photographs, and measure and map the location of all finds, samples, and features. Excavations require reams of notes, drawings, and other paperwork. The director must keep an excavation log or diary, recording the course of the excavations, the

A busy excavation.

work schedule, the number of people working, accounts of expenses, dimensions and positioning of excavation areas, layout of the measuring system, and all the finds. There must be recording systems for all measurements, for observations and interpretations, and for all drawings, photos, and samples.

The director must monitor progress in the field laboratory as well, where finds are washed, sorted, cataloged, and bagged for storage. Some knowledge of preservation techniques is necessary to protect fragile objects. The director also needs to be able to deal with people and social relationships under demanding conditions in field camps. The excavation director needs to be a jack-of-all-trades to be successful. At the same time, no one can be an expert in all the different kinds of information needed to study archaeological sites and artifacts. Excavation directors rely heavily on specialists in geology, zoology, botany, preservation, and the like.

Records

THE FIELD CREW

Excavation is a labor-intensive undertaking, and the field crew is the most important part of the project. This group of individuals is involved in the actual digging process, unearthing the sites and artifacts. Crews are composed of a variety of individuals, young and old, ranging from professional archaeologists with advanced degrees, to undergraduate and graduate students, and sometimes just people interested in the subject. Archaeology is the science of the past, but it is also a social experience in the present.

Fieldwork can require a few days, weeks, or months, walking miles each day with your head down in survey of the ground, or moving tons of earth to expose buried levels. Excavations are hard work, often in the hot sun. Frequently they are carried out in remote places, requiring patience and endurance. Archaeology is also good dirty fun, and the experience of working, and relaxing, with others who enjoy the same things can be unforgettable. The discovery process is captivating, and sharing that excitement with colleagues and comrades enhances the entire experience.

Fieldwork

Finally, fieldwork is an extraordinary learning experience. One realizes the difficulties involved in recovering information from the past and comes to appreciate how much has been learned. In addition, a constant stream of questions about the past and the significance of place, artifact, and context come to mind while in the field. All in all, archaeological fieldwork can be one of the most stimulating activities there is.

This excavation began with the removal of the plowzone by shoveling and screening the earth to expose the intact soil beneath. (Courtesy of Michael Kienitz.)

SELECTING SITES FOR EXCAVATION

Site Choice

The choice of which site to excavate is determined by several factors, including potential danger to the archaeological remains. Sites are often chosen for excavation because they appear to be well preserved or to contain new information that will give further insight into the prehistory of a particular region. The choice of a site for excavation is often based on the results of a survey or testing. An initial survey of an area, including coring and testing of promising sites, might indicate that one or several sites would be worth excavating. Careful surface collection and testing must be carried out at the site selected for excavation in order to make sure the site can provide the kinds of information that are needed and to assist in planning the excavation.

Site Destruction

Archaeological sites are being destroyed at a rapid rate by the growth and development of modern civilization. There is a serious and real concern about the loss of undisturbed sites for future research. Sites threatened by modern construction are often good candidates for excavation.

One branch of archaeology is concerned primarily with evaluation of the impact of such construction and the rescue of threatened archaeological and historical materials. Cultural Resource Management (CRM) is the name given to this activity. Areas where construction or building activities are planned must be inspected by archaeologists to determine if there are significant cultural resources present. If such remains are detected, the archaeologists record and sometimes excavate the materials in order to save them from destruction. A large number of archaeologists in the United States and other countries are employed in both government and private businesses to conduct such environmental impact studies.

Cultural Resource Management

It is important to know as much as possible about a site prior to full-scale excavation in order to choose the best strategy for the project. At every excavation, the archaeologist is faced with a series of decisions about how to achieve the most and best-documented information under the given circumstances. Ideally, a site could be fully excavated and everything recorded in the finest detail. Realistically, however, constraints on time and funding, as well as a desire to leave a portion of the site for future archaeologists, make it standard practice to excavate only a portion of the total site. Accurate notes and records of the layers, structures, and artifacts at a site are essential, not only for the investigator, but also to create a permanent archive of information about the site that is available to others.

Excavation Strategy

A deep excavation in waterlogged deposits.

MAPS AND GRIDS

Site Grid

Accurate mapping of layers and artifacts is the key to the proper recording of information at an archaeological excavation. A grid is marked out across the surface of a site prior to the excavation to be used for all horizontal measurements. A **site grid** represents a coordinate system, with lines typically running north–south and east–west at regular intervals. Intervals along the two axes of the grid are designated with a system of letters or numbers or both. The grid lines and measurements within each grid square are measured as distances in meters and centimeters north and east of the base lines at the edge of the excavations.

The site grid might also be oriented according to local topography or archaeological features such as mounds or middens. For example, at coastal sites, trenches are sometimes excavated perpendicular to the coastline in order to study stratigraphy and site formation in relation to the coast. In a narrow cave, the grid is often aligned to the long axis of the cave.

The Datum

Location of the site and the site grid in relation to global latitude and longitude must be determined. A control point, or site **datum,** must be located near the excavation as a point of origin for vertical measurements. A preexisting datum point like a surveyor's benchmark may be used if available. Otherwise, a permanent feature like a rock outcrop or building foundation might be marked and used as the datum point. The location and elevation of this point must be established in relation to known points like geographic features or distant landmarks.

Recording Measurements

Vertical location in the excavation is best determined using a surveying instrument, set at a known elevation, and sighting on a vertical measuring rod. Measurements at the site should be converted to meters above sea level, or the elevation of the datum line may simply be recorded. Modern surveying instruments, known as **total stations,** that employ GPS (global positioning satellites), a radio survey system, and computerized display have greatly improved mapping and measurement in archaeology.

TEST PITS

Testing

Preliminary examination of a site involves making a few small excavations to preview the site. Testing the site normally involves small-scale excavations to determine the presence, quantity, and extent of archaeological materials. These test excavations can be small, vertical test pits,

Excavation of a long trench reveals distinct layers.

perhaps a square meter in size, or a series of one or more trenches across the site. The test squares to be excavated might also be placed in rows or in a checkerboard pattern across the site, or their location might be chosen by random sampling as described in Chapter 6.

The size and number of test pits to be excavated depends on the kind of information being sought. In some cases, it is difficult to visualize the **stratigraphy,** or set of layers, observed in the small test pits. One or two long trenches across the site may provide a better view of the stratigraphy.

VERTICAL EXCAVATIONS

Excavations are generally either vertical or horizontal. Vertical excavation takes the form of squares or rectangles carefully positioned across a site to expose stratigraphy and artifact contents. By studying the vertical walls (the **sections**) of these excavations, the investigator can observe buried layers in the earth.

What do these *layers mean?*

Stratigraphy

The stratigraphy of natural sediments and human deposits reveals how the site was formed and accumulated. The relationships between deposits in the stratigraphic sequence indicate the chronological arrangement of the layers. The bottom layer is deposited first as the oldest layer in the sequence. The subsequent layers are progressively younger. Thus, the stratigraphic sequence provides a relative chronology whereby layers and the artifacts they contain can be determined to be "younger" or "older" than other layers and artifacts in the same sequence.

The thickness of a layer is not determined so much by the length of time that it took to accumulate, but by the natural and human activities involved in the deposition of the materials. For example, heaps of shells may accumulate very rapidly into high shell middens; the collapse of houses with earth or sod walls results in very thick layers; stone tool manufacture can produce extensive debris. On the other hand, the place where an animal was killed and butchered—a kill site—may leave almost no archaeological trace.

Evaluation of a stratigraphic sequence involves distinguishing between natural and human activities. Environmental factors like soil erosion or flood deposits may add to the local accumulation, but may also remove part of a layer. More recent features like postholes or storage pits may have been dug into older deposits. The relationship between layers must be studied carefully to determine whether younger deposits are cut into older layers and whether disturbances like animal activities, downed trees, floods, or later construction have disturbed or destroyed the original stratigraphy.

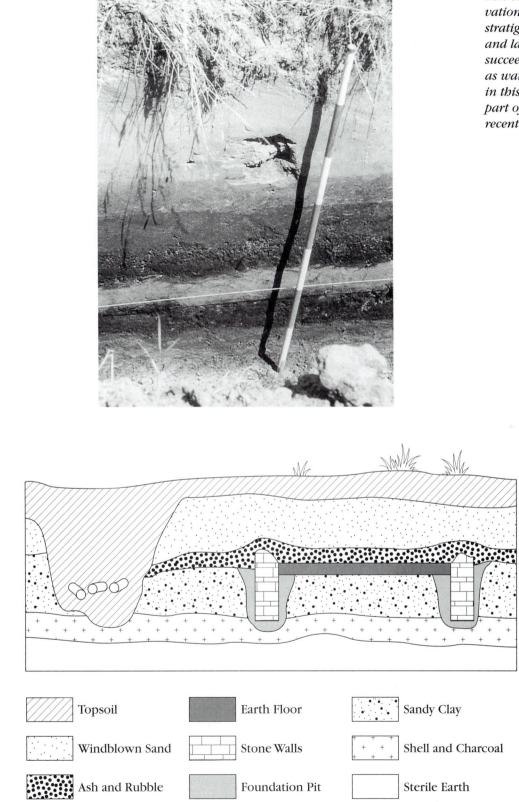

This section of an excavation trench exposes a stratigraphy of stream and lake deposits that succeeded one another as water levels changed in this area. The upper part of the deposit is recent blown sand.

Topsoil

Windblown Sand

Ash and Rubble

Earth Floor

Stone Walls

Foundation Pit

Sandy Clay

Shell and Charcoal

Sterile Earth

Assessment of the context and relative position of layers allows an archaeologist to interpret the depositional history from the stratigraphic sequence. An approximate date of the layers may be derived from artifacts of a known age found in a particular layer. For example, a hubcap from a 1935 Ford would indicate that the layer could date back no earlier than 1935. The ages of many types of pottery and stone tools are also known and can be used to suggest an approximate date for archaeological levels. Layers sometimes may also be dated by means of absolute techniques like **radiocarbon dating,** discussed in Chapter 3.

The drawing of site stratigraphy on page 29 shows a hypothetical example of a sequence of deposits in the ground, involving three different episodes of human activity. By careful study and analysis of the layers, it is possible to determine the sequence of events that took place here. The basal layer of sterile earth was first covered in prehistory by a layer of shells and charcoal that accumulated as a midden comprised of the remains of shellfish like clams or mussels. This shell layer was then covered naturally by sandy clay, deposited by a river flood.

Later, a brick house was built on top of the sandy clay layer. The foundation trenches for the house walls were cut through the sandy clay and into the older midden beneath. The house was destroyed by fire. A dark

layer of ash and rubble covered the area in and around the house. Subsequently, a sandstorm buried the place completely in a thick layer. Next, the growth of vegetation created a layer of topsoil in the upper part of the sand layer. Most recently, a pit was dug into the topsoil, through the sand, the house remains, the sandy clay, and into the midden deposit. The pit was then filled with trash and topsoil.

Chapter 2 Archaeological Excavation

A horizontal excavation. Only one half of a feature is excavated at first. This feature, a house depression, is being excavated with trowels. The small wall in the middle is kept as a record of the feature's stratigraphy. Artifacts, bones, and other finds are mapped by layer. (Courtesy of Michael Kienitz.)

HORIZONTAL, OR AREA, EXCAVATIONS

Features

Horizontal, or area, excavations expose large open areas of ground, one layer at a time. Area excavations are intended to recover information on site arrangement and structures. Such excavations may expose actual prehistoric living floors where a group of people carried out everyday activities. Human activities in the past often included digging, construction, burning, burial, and the like. Such visible changes in the ground at an archaeological site are called **features.** Other types of features include fireplaces, storage pits, walls, and graves.

Holes often are dug in the ground to insert wooden posts for construction. Such **postholes** provide a great deal of information on the nature of structures and site arrangement. A complex network of postholes or walls may appear within an excavated area, revealing the outline of houses, fences, or other structures. A series of postholes filled with one kind of soil to the same depth can be connected to indicate a single stage of construction. If postholes filled with one type of soil were dug into postholes with another kind of soil, the former would likely be the result of a different phase or period of construction.

Horizontal Exposures

When the site stratigraphy is relatively simple—with only one or two stages of occupation and thin layers of artifacts and other materials—it

Excavations expose post-holes and the foundations of two houses, one built over the other. The dark rectangles mark the location of construction posts. Two fireplace pits can be seen at the center and right of the photo. (Courtesy of Dr. James B. Stoltman.)

is possible to separate the remains from each stage of occupation. In such cases, it is advantageous to expose large surfaces of the same layer to get an overview of the distribution of features and artifacts. Following removal of the topsoil, the surface is scraped with trowels or shovels, loose soil is removed, and features and artifacts are uncovered. The uncovered surface is then carefully recorded, usually in photographs, drawings, and maps of the size and location of features and other important information. The excavated soils are usually sifted through screens and/or washed with water to find even the smallest objects, fragments of bone, and plant remains.

The surface should also be recorded in a drawing, with important objects numbered individually. A separate catalog can then be made of all the artifacts, with their inventory number, type of material, kind of artifact, location, and layer. The recorded objects are removed one at a time and put in bags with a label showing their number.

Recording Information

A variety of samples are taken from different layers in the walls of the excavation and from the occupation floor. Soil samples are taken to help define and characterize the deposits at the site. Pollen samples are sometimes taken to assist in defining the vegetation in and around the site. Samples of charcoal and bone are taken for radiocarbon dating at most sites.

Samples

The surface of the sediments beneath the occupation layer is uncovered and cleaned. Unusual colors in the soil may reveal features such as

The excavations in progress. The long stadia rod is used to measure the depth of an artifact.

Water-screening the artifacts is a large part of the work of excavation.

The stones and bones found in the screen.

Items are washed, dried, and put in bags with labels showing their location in the site. (Courtesy of Michael Kienitz.)

pits and postholes; these are recorded in photos and drawings. Features are normally dissected by excavating one quarter or one half of the pit or posthole at a time in order to remove the contents and determine the function of the feature. This produces a vertical section through the middle of the feature and allows a view of how it was formed.

AFTER THE DIG

At the end of the dig, the excavation has to be filled up and undisturbed portions of the site protected in the best possible manner. Records, artifacts, and samples must be shipped back to the home laboratory to be cataloged and prepared for analysis. After the fieldwork come more detailed analyses of the recovered materials, the writing of excavation reports, and the preparation of publications, all of which require more work and time than the excavation itself.

Publication

Final results of the investigations are made available to the public and to professional archaeologists through articles in popular and scientific journals and published reports. More about analysis and interpretation in archaeological investigations appears in the next chapter.

A FINAL NOTE

Historical archives may be studied over and over again, but archaeological sites are nonrenewable resources. Excavations involve removing the earth and all its contents. Every excavation means the destruction of all or part of an archaeological site. One of the advantages of Fugawiland is that you can learn about excavating without destroying anything.

All that is left when an excavation is over are the finds themselves, the unexcavated parts of the site, and the samples, photographs, drawings, measurements, and other notes that the archaeologists made. Accurate notes and records of the layers, structures, and finds at a site are essential, not only for the investigator but also as a permanent archive of information about the site.

For these reasons, excavations should always be done under the direction of professional archaeologists, who are trained to conduct investigations that accurately record information, to preserve and protect the materials that are uncovered, and to publish what they learn. Information that is not recorded properly during the removal of archaeological materials is lost forever.

CHAPTER 3

~~~~~~

ANALYSIS AND INTERPRETATION

When the fieldwork is over, the materials collected in surveys and excavations must be cleaned, classified, counted, cataloged, and analyzed. Archaeological fieldwork produces several major categories of materials and information: (1) **artifacts,** portable objects altered by human activity, (2) **ecofacts,** the remains of plants, animals, sediments, and other unmodified materials that result from human activity, (3) **features,** the immovable structures, layers, pits, and posts in the ground, and (4) **sites and settlements,** the set of artifacts, ecofacts, and features that define places in the landscape where activity and residence were focused. These categories are described below along with a discussion of dating methods in archaeology.

The Postfieldwork Process

A variety of specialists are needed to examine and interpret the wide range of materials and information that are found at archaeological sites. Lithic specialists analyze stone tools, and ceramic specialists study sherds of ancient pottery. Paleoethnobotanists study plant remains, both visible and microscopic. Archaeozoologists investigate animal bones, which represent the remains of meals and manufacturing activities. Physical anthropologists and human osteologists describe and interpret human bones and teeth. Geoarchaeologists and micromorphologists investigate the geological setting of the site and the details of the sediments encasing the archaeological remains. Archaeological remains are defined in terms of their location in time and space. Dating methods are used to determine the age of remains. Archaeometrists date those remains and can determine the chemical characterization of prehistoric materials to learn about their composition and source.

Specialists

The analysis and interpretation of archaeological remains is intended to better our understanding of past human society. Some of the important concerns in such studies that are relevant to Fugawiland include

Excavation reveals a small pottery vessel in the bottom of the pit.

technology and subsistence, social organization, and ideology. These topics are considered in the last sections of this chapter.

ARTIFACTS

The Catalog

Each object from the excavation must be washed to remove dust and dirt. In some projects, each object is recorded by number in a catalog of the finds. At other sites, artifacts are recorded by material and context, or by the excavation area where they were found. Numbering artifacts with permanent ink ensures that each has a label with information on the site and location of the find.

The catalog description of each artifact includes a record of the kind of artifact, the type of raw material, the color, the overall shape and measurements, techniques of manufacturing, presumed function, decoration, and information on location. This description could be supplemented with an accurate drawing and a photograph of the artifact. An inventory of the materials from the excavation then can be made by

Sorting and cataloging artifacts and other finds from an excavation. (Courtesy of Michael Kienitz.)

counting and recording the number of artifacts in each category of material, such as chipped stone, ground stone, or pottery.

Following this initial recording, artifacts are classified into other categories and types. **Classification** is the process of dividing objects into groups on the basis of shared characteristics. One example of such classification is the initial division of the remains into artifacts, ecofacts, and features, described earlier. Another example would be the division of chipped stone artifacts into such categories as axes, scrapers, knives, or arrowheads.

Classification

Several primary attributes are used to classify archaeological artifacts: (1) **form,** the size and basic shape of the object, (2) **function,** the presumed or known use of the artifact, (3) **technology,** the characteristics of raw materials and manufacturing techniques, and (4) **style,** the color, texture, and decoration of the object. Most of this information is recorded in the laboratory after the artifacts have been cleaned and cataloged.

Artifact Attributes

ECOFACTS

Ecofacts are natural items, such as animal bones and plant remains, usually brought to the site by its occupants and useful for the study of past human activity. Ecofacts can be used to reconstruct the former environment of the site and the range of resources that the inhabitants used. Ecofacts are classified as organic (plants and animals) or inorganic (sediments and stone). These materials are usually studied by archaeologists or specialists with training in botany, zoology, or geology.

Pollen

Plant remains from an archaeological site may include pollen, seeds, leaves, pieces of wood, and the like, depending on the quality of preservation. Microscopic **pollen** is usually wind-deposited and may be introduced naturally to the site. Each type of plant produces distinctive pollen. Because of its long-distance distribution, pollen is likely to reflect the total environment around the site.

Changes in the types of pollen at a site over time can be used to reconstruct the vegetational history of the area and to provide a record of climatic changes. Special growing requirements and other characteristics of certain plants may reflect certain climatic conditions or specific local situations like an open versus a forested environment around a site.

Plant Remains

Macrofossils are visible remains of botanical materials like seeds and plant parts that are more likely to be present at a site due to direct human utilization. Identification of these remains indicates what species of plants were present, whether they were wild or domestic, and in what context they were found. It is important to study the context of these remains to know how the plants were used. Plants may be collected for food, but they may also be used for production of textiles, mats, and baskets; for making poison for arrowheads; or as drugs. Types of plants and their growing conditions may also indicate the nature of the local environment and climate.

Animal Bones

Faunal analysis, or archaeozoology, refers to studies of the animal remains from archaeological sites. Animal remains are tabulated by the kinds of bones, teeth, antlers, and horns that are present. Species are identified, and the numbers of individuals of each species are calculated. These studies show what animals were hunted and eaten and in what proportion. The amount of meat available from each animal also might be calculated to determine their relative importance in the diet.

Age and Sex

Faunal analysis also can provide an estimate of the ratio of adult to juvenile animals and of male to female animals. A predominance of certain age groups in a species such as deer may indicate that seasonal or selective hunting was practiced. For example, a site that contained a large proportion of three- to six-month old deer would suggest the animals were killed primarily in the fall because deer are born in the spring.

The presence or absence of certain parts of the animal skeleton may indicate the way animals were butchered and whether they were

Animal bones from archaeological sites.

Broken bones and a flint blade in the place where they were found.

dismembered on the spot or killed elsewhere and selected steaks and chops brought back to the settlement. Not all animals are necessarily hunted for food. Nonfood items such as antlers, fur, bones, and hides are also important materials from hunted animals.

Soils and Sediments

The most important inorganic ecofacts are the various sediments uncovered by excavation. Deposits of soils and sediments at human settlements result from both human and natural processes. These sediments and deposits are studied by geoarchaeologists. The type of sediments present might indicate the source of the material that was deposited. Examples include water-lain silts from a flood, volcanic ashes, or frost-cracked rocks from the ceiling of a cave. The study of soil chemistry is an important aspect of the analysis of soils and sediments.

FEATURES

Features must be studied largely in the field since they are fixed in the ground. Features may be structures like houses or pits; or fences or field

Features at the site are recorded in drawings and photographs.

systems defining an area used for special purposes; or constructions for certain activities like drying racks, fireplaces, and traps. Features are useful for understanding the distribution and organization of human activities at a site. For example, the size, elaboration, and location of houses or burials may suggest differences in wealth and status.

Some features result from the accumulation of garbage and debris, rather than being intentionally constructed. Such features include shell **middens** (large dumps of shell from mussels, oysters, or other species), heaps of waste material in workshops, and quarries. Studies of these features may indicate strategies for obtaining food or raw material, how the raw material was used and distributed, and whether it was scarce or abundant.

Burials and human bones are a special category of feature often found at archaeological sites. Several different kinds of burials can be identified. Simple **inhumations,** or **extended burials,** represent the laid-out burial of the whole body. Such graves usually contain an articulated skeleton, with all the bones in their correct position. **Secondary burials** are the result of burial of some of the skeleton, after the flesh and soft tissue has disappeared. Usually, the skull and larger bones are present, often in a small pile or bundle. **Cremations** are burials of the ash and small carbonized bones from bodies that have been burned prior to burial.

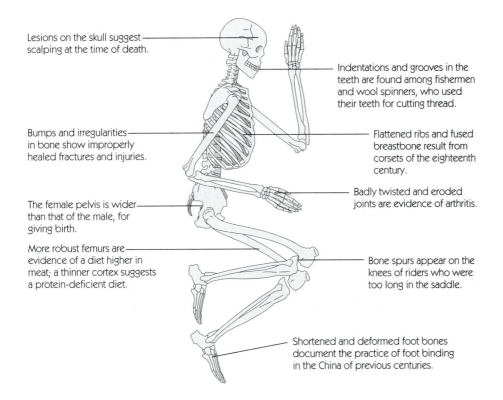

Lesions on the skull suggest scalping at the time of death.

Indentations and grooves in the teeth are found among fishermen and wool spinners, who used their teeth for cutting thread.

Bumps and irregularities in bone show improperly healed fractures and injuries.

Flattened ribs and fused breastbone result from corsets of the eighteenth century.

The female pelvis is wider than that of the male, for giving birth.

Badly twisted and eroded joints are evidence of arthritis.

More robust femurs are evidence of a diet higher in meat; a thinner cortex suggests a protein-deficient diet.

Bone spurs appear on the knees of riders who were too long in the saddle.

Shortened and deformed foot bones document the practice of foot binding in the China of previous centuries.

An excavated grave.

Analysis of Burials

Osteologists are concerned with the identification and analysis of such human remains. The sex of the skeleton can be determined by the size and shape of the pelvis and the skull and the thickness of the bones. The age of death can be estimated by the eruption sequence and wear of the teeth, the **fusion** (closing) of sutures between bones of the skull, and the fusion of the ends of the limb bones to the shaft.

Disease and Trauma

The health status of past populations can be investigated by recording the incidence of trauma and malnutrition that affects the skeleton. Such diseases and injuries include bone fractures, arthritis, and periodontal diseases. Nutritional problems may be reflected in poorly developed bones and the low average height of the population. Cultural practices like cranial deformation or dental mutilation, practiced in prehistoric America, also show up in the skeletal remains.

Federal and state laws exist for the protection of human burials. It is also the case that some Native American groups in North America do not want archaeologists to disturb the remains of their ancestors. The best policy is to contact state and local authorities prior to any excavation involving human remains.

SITES AND SETTLEMENTS

Settlement archaeology is the study of how and why prehistoric remains are distributed across the landscape. Investigations range from the analysis of the location of different activities within a single room to the distribution of sites in a region. Usually, three levels of locational information are investigated: (1) a single structure or occupation surface such as a cave floor, (2) a site or settlement, or (3) a series of sites within a larger region.

The spatial organization within a single structure defines areas for special activities such as grinding flour, cooking, weaving, and manufacturing tools or for certain facilities such as sleeping areas or storage. Such studies may indicate a division of male and female space and activities, how many people lived in a household, and the structure of the family—nuclear, extended, or polygynous, for example.

Structures

A **settlement** generally includes a habitation area with one or more houses and fireplaces; different activity areas for tasks such as preparing food, curing animal skins and hides, and manufacturing various artifacts, perhaps storage equipment; and a midden or trash area. Spatial patterning within a site can provide information about the number of houses and people at the settlement and on their relationships with one another. In addition, most of the day-to-day activities of the occupants should be reflected in the various structures and activity areas found throughout the settlement. Structures at a site may be solid and substantial in the case of permanently settled communities in a villagelike or townlike setting. Short-term or seasonal settlements, however, may leave little trace of construction.

Settlements

The size of a settlement in terms of horizontal and vertical extent depends on the number of people living there, the length of time they lived there, and the kinds of activities they performed and structures they erected, as well as environmental factors. Sites of similar size could have been created by a few permanently settled people or through the occasional use of the same spot by a larger group of people.

Differences in the size and architectural elaboration of houses may be evidence of status differentiation, a situation whereby some people have more wealth and control over goods and labor than others. The arrangement of houses in a settlement also may reflect social organization in the separation of poor and wealthy households. Concerns for privacy and protection in the form of fences, palisades, or ditches may indicate private ownership or conditions of competition or warfare. Settlement studies also may reveal areas of economic specialization, with certain materials produced by skilled craftsmen and other items made in individual households.

Regional settlement patterns that are recorded in archaeological surveys can provide a variety of information on the prehistoric use of the landscape. Several different kinds of sites may be found in an area. Residential

Regions

settlements of various size and duration are typical targets for investigation. Such sites can vary from camps to villages, towns, and even cities.

There are many other kinds of sites. **Extraction sites** are used for more specific, nonresidential purposes to obtain raw materials or resources, such as quarries for stone or copper or places where animals were killed and butchered. Distinct burial areas, outside of settlements, are another kind of site. Examples include cemeteries of inhumation graves, cremation urns, and individual burial mounds and tombs.

ARCHAEOLOGICAL DATING

Relative Dating

It is always important to know the age of prehistoric sites so we can place them in time and determine the sequence of past events. Archaeologists distinguish between relative and absolute dates. **Relative** dates provide an estimate of the age of an object in relation to other objects, but do not provide an exact date. For example, we can say that wagon wheels are usually older than car tires, or that the Egyptian pyramids are older than the White House, without stating a specific age.

Stratigraphic Dating

Stratigraphic sequences provide a relative chronology of geological layers from older at the bottom to younger at the top. A deep stratified deposit may allow the archaeologist to determine a temporal sequence for a number of different periods. A relative chronology makes it possible to study changes in the artifacts over time and observe temporal trends of change. Ordering artifacts in a relative chronology is a big step toward establishing a temporal framework. However, a relative chronology does not provide the actual age of an object nor can it tell us how much time is involved in calendar years.

Absolute Dating

Absolute dating methods assign a specific calendar age to an object in years before the present (B.P.), which can be converted to B.C. (before Christ) or A.D. (anno domini) calendar years. For example, the great Egyptian pyramid of Khufu at Giza dates to around 2500 B.C. and the White House to A.D. 1800.

Dating in calendar years (**absolute chronology**) is possible if artifacts can be related to historical events. For example, a coin showing the face of a certain king or containing an inscribed date found inside a house provides an approximate age for the house because the house cannot be older the coin. However, a large part of the archaeological record is older than historical records or coinage and cannot be dated using such information.

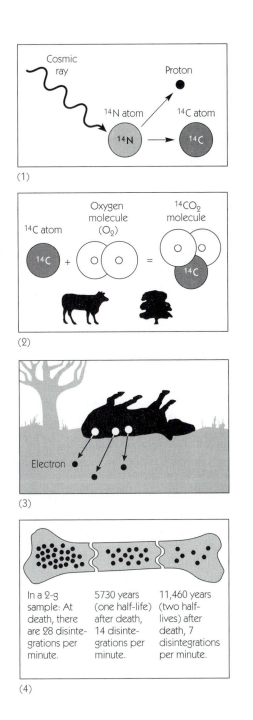

(1)

(2)

(3)

(4)

The principles of radiocarbon dating. Source: T. Douglas Price and Gary M. Feinman, Images of the Past, *3rd ed. (Mountain View, CA: Mayfield, 2001), p. 142.*

One of the best methods for determining the absolute age of prehistoric materials is **radiocarbon dating,** based on the principle of radioactive decay. Unstable radioactive isotopes in various materials decay into stable isotopes over a known amount of time. The unstable, radioactive isotope of carbon (carbon-14 or ^{14}C) is produced in the atmosphere as a result of cosmic radiation. Carbon-14 is a very rare commodity, and only

Radiocarbon Dating

about 6 kilograms (13 pounds) are produced each year. There are only about 60 tons on earth. Carbon-14 is distributed evenly in the atmosphere and combines with oxygen in the same way as normal carbon to form carbon dioxide.

All living things absorb both stable carbon (primarily ^{12}C) and its radioactive isotope (^{14}C) throughout their lifetime. Plants incorporate carbon dioxide through photosynthesis, and animals eat plants or other animals. The proportion of ^{12}C and ^{14}C remains constant in an organism, as in the atmosphere, until its death, when the intake of fresh carbon stops.

Following the death of the organism, the amount of radioactive carbon in the tissue of the organism begins to decay—that is, the ratio of ^{14}C to ^{12}C begins to decrease at a constant rate. The rate of decay for ^{14}C has a half-life of about 5730 years. This means that a sample containing 15 grams of ^{14}C has only 7.5 grams after a period of 5730 years; after 11,460 years, only 3.75 grams remain; and so on. Thus, the amount of ^{14}C left in ancient plant or animal remains may be used to determine the time elapsed since death. The difference between the original amount of ^{14}C and the present amount is used to calculate the age of the sample in calendar years. Because of the potential errors in counting radiocarbon, dates are always given with a plus/minus value to indicate that the actual date probably falls within the range indicated. A radiocarbon measurement of 2250 ±50 years before present means the date of the object probably falls between 2200 and 2300 years ago. All radiocarbon dates before present are calculated from A.D. 1950, so 2200 and 2300 years ago in calendar years was 150–250 B.C.

A variety of organic materials can be measured by radiocarbon dating including wood, bone, shell, charcoal, antler, and other items. Carbon-14 often survives best at prehistoric sites in the form of charcoal, and this material has been most commonly dated by the radiocarbon dating method. However, wood charcoal can come from very old trees or wood and may not date the actual archaeological material accurately. If charcoal from the inner rings of an old tree is used, the date the tree was cut may be off by several hundred years. For more reliable dates, plants other than trees should be used. Materials with a short life such as nutshells, corncobs, small twigs are preferred over wood charcoal.

Determining the amount of ^{14}C remaining in prehistoric materials is not an easy task. It's like locating a specific piece of gravel in a full dump truck. Careful laboratory procedures and expensive scientific equipment are needed to measure the amount of ^{14}C in a sample. A sample of known weight is carefully cleaned and then burned to create a pure gas of carbon dioxide. The radioactive carbon isotopes in that gas are then counted. In simple terms, a Geiger counter is used to record individual radioactive decay or emissions from the gas. Several grams of organic material are normally required to produce enough gas for counting.

In the last two decades, however, technology has greatly improved in radiocarbon dating. Accelerator mass spectrometry (AMS) has replaced the Geiger counter method. AMS involves the separation and counting of individual carbon atoms by their weight, a much more accurate process. Much smaller samples can be measured much more quickly than before. Less than 0.01 gram of sample is needed, and individual pieces of charcoal, a single nutshell, or a cereal grain can be dated directly. AMS dating is now being used to provide dates from many sites and materials that could not be measured previously.

Radiocarbon dating was originally based on the assumption that there had been no changes in the amount of ^{14}C in the atmosphere over time. However, radiocarbon dating of tree rings of known age has shown that this assumption was not correct and that radiocarbon dates underestimated the actual age of a sample. To make up for this error, dates in radiocarbon years are now calculated, or **calibrated,** to correct calendar years using a formula or a graph such as the one shown here. (This graph is only an example of a calibration curve and is not intended for use except in Fugawiland.)

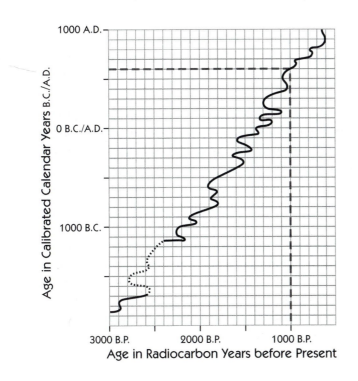

A vertical line is drawn from the bottom of the graph (radiocarbon years before present) up to the wavy line. From that point, a line is drawn horizontally to the left of the graph to obtain the correct age in calendar years B.C. or A.D. For example, a radiocarbon date of 1000 years B.P. would be corrected to A.D. 600 using the graph, as shown by the heavy, dashed line. The corrected date is known as a calibrated date and is a more accurate age for the sample than radiocarbon years B.P. You might note that some vertical lines drawn through the graph can intersect the curve in two or more places. In such situations, the accuracy of the radiocarbon dating is less certain.

RECONSTRUCTING PAST SOCIETIES

Archaeological information that is recovered from the ground, and described and analyzed by specialists, does not directly tell us very much about the past. The analysis may tell us what kinds of objects were made, what they were made of, how they were used, and how old they are. But the questions that archaeologists seek to answer concern larger concepts about the way of life of prehistoric peoples, how human societies coped with their physical and social environments, and how our predecessors viewed their world. Both the questions we ask and the ideas we use to find the answers are at the heart of interpretation in archaeology. The science of archaeology lies in bridging that gap between the information we recover and the questions we seek to answer.

The kinds of questions that archaeologists ask about past societies in general terms involve technology, economy, social organization, and ideology.

Technology

Technology is the set of techniques and knowledge that allows people to convert natural resources into tools, food, clothing, shelter, and other products and equipment they need or want. Technology is the means by which people interact directly with their natural environment. It is also the aspect of past culture that is most easily observed in archaeological data. The fragments of the tools that people used in the past, made of durable materials such as stone, ceramic, and metal, are the most common archaeological remains. Changes in technology over time provide clear indicators of the development of our cultural means of adaptation.

Economy and Subsistence

Economy concerns how people obtain foods, material, and goods to sustain their lives. One major aspect of prehistoric economies was **subsistence**—the activities and materials by which people feed themselves. Archaeologists use the term *subsistence pattern* to describe the plants and animals that prehistoric people ate, the activities required to obtain those foods, and the procurement and preparation techniques and implements used to turn those plants and animals into food. Hunting and gathering describes one such pattern in which wild animals are hunted and wild plants are collected or gathered for subsistence. Agriculture, another form of subsistence, involves herding domesticated animals and cultivating domesticated plants.

Exchange is another aspect of economy. When artifacts such as stone axes, obsidian knives, metal spear-points, or certain kinds of food have passed from person to person, archaeologists talk about "exchange." One way to study interaction within and between societies is to look at the distribution of items of exchange. Economic anthropologists distinguish three different kinds of exchange: reciprocity, redistribution, and trade. **Reciprocal exchange** usually takes the form of gift-giving, whereby objects of relatively equal value are given to build alliances. **Redistribution** involves the movement of goods to a central place from which they are portioned out to members of the society. Such a system of redistribution might be used to support an army, or priests, or the pyramid builders of ancient Egypt.

Large-scale economic transactions known as **trade** often involve some sort of market economy, perhaps a monetary standard. Trade takes place in our own economic system today—objects are imported and exported for the purpose of making a profit. This level of exchange usually involves a highly complex society with professional artisans, regular supplies of raw material, extensive transportation systems, protection of markets and traders against pirates, and enough customers to make the business worthwhile.

Archaeologists often examine exchange and interaction through the study of **"exotic materials."** The presence of objects and materials that are not available or locally produced in the study area provides immediate evidence of connections and interaction with others. Of greatest use in such investigations are artifacts or materials that come from a single location. An example of the use and exchange of different raw materials is seen in Fugawiland.

Social organization refers to the roles and relationships in society and concerns relations between women and men and among different segments of society, such as families, different age groups, labor units, and ethnic groups. Organization structures various aspects of society such as social interaction, economic activity, and political relationships.

Kinship and marriage systems, lineage, **sodality,** rank, and class are important aspects of social organization and a means of structuring

Exchange

Trade

Exotic Materials

Social Organization

social relationships. Kinship defines the relationship between individual members in society on the basis of their family relationships. Grandmother, brother, uncle, and cousin are terms that relate us to other people through kinship. Marriage systems tie unrelated individuals together through sanctioned kinship; rules for these relationships are carefully defined in society. Lineages provide a means for calculating one's relationships through lines of ancestry. Such genealogies are a way to extend relationships and determine membership in a group. Members of the same lineage often work as a corporate group.

Rank and Class

Rank and class distinguish groups of people within most societies. Many societies of hunter-gatherers are described as egalitarian, with equal relations between all members of the group, lacking strong rank or class distinctions. Many agricultural societies, on the other hand, exhibit distinctive groups within the society that are defined by inherited status differences. Higher status (resulting from prestige, wealth, and/or power) characterizes elite and privileged groups in a society. Rank and class are means of defining such status groups. Rank refers to inherited positions in societies in which everyone is ranked in terms of status relative to all other people. The firstborn of the highest ranked group is the highest position in such a society. In ranked societies, each individual has a unique place in the order of relationships. Class societies are structured by distinctions between groups, or classes, of people that define levels, or strata, in society. Class, which is usually inherited, defines large groups of individuals and may determine one's job, location of residence, marriage opportunities, and financial status. The former caste system of India provides an extreme example of a society structured by class.

Division of Labor

The economic activities of prehistoric peoples were organized in different ways. A fundamental mechanism for the organization of tasks is the division of labor. Separate groups or segments of society undertake different activities as part of the economic process. A basic example is seen in many groups of hunter-gatherers where the division of labor is by sex; males are primarily hunters and females are primarily gatherers. This doesn't mean that men don't gather and women don't sometimes hunt, but in general subsistence activities are organized along the lines of gender. Both groups contribute foodstuffs to the subsistence economy of the group. Agricultural societies also see economic organization along gender lines, but the household becomes an important component of production for food and other necessary materials. Production becomes more specialized over time, with entire communities involved in producing specific items or the emergence of specialist groups of producers such as potters, metalsmiths, and bead makers. Production can assume more formal structures such as guilds or unions in larger, more complex societies.

In a general sense, political organization reflects the increasing complexity in human society over time. As societies became larger, organizational changes took place that resulted in closer integration and more linear decision making.

One of the most significant changes in organization was the shift from egalitarian to hierarchical structures that often followed the origins of agriculture. Hierarchical organizations have one or more levels of control above the majority of the people in the society. These higher levels are seen in elite classes or ranks that control much of the wealth, power, and decision making in the society. One way to imagine such a hierarchy is to recall the nature of military organization and the chain of command from privates to lieutenants to generals. Privates report to corporals and sergeants, sergeants report to lieutenants, lieutenants report to colonels, and so forth. Specific details and requests flow from the bottom of the ladder upward; general information and commands flow down.

Government operates in a hierarchical manner as well, from local representatives to municipal government, state government, and federal government. The sphere of control and decision making varies with the level in the hierarchy. The municipal government repairs local roads, the federal government builds an interstate system.

There are a number of ways to describe or characterize such hierarchies in human society. One of the most common terminologies uses the concepts of bands, tribes, chiefdoms, and states to distinguish different kinds of political organization. Bands and tribes describe relatively small societies of hunter-gatherers or farmers in which relationships are generally egalitarian and decision making is consensual. Power and property are distributed among all the members of the population. Status is earned through achievements and is ephemeral, held only by the individual who gained it. Chiefdoms and states are larger, often territorial, societies in which relationships are unequal and organization is hierarchical. Status is hereditary and assigned or ascribed by birth order or class affiliation.

One of the more apparent (though not always present) trends in the organization of human society is an increase in complexity over time. Complexity refers to the development of more units in society and more integration between those units. More units are a result of social, economic, and ideological specialization. Such differentiation is reflected in the distinctions among villages, towns, and cities that began to appear with chiefdoms and states. More integration is a result of hierarchical

Hierarchy

Complexity

Types of societies and the appearance of institutions.

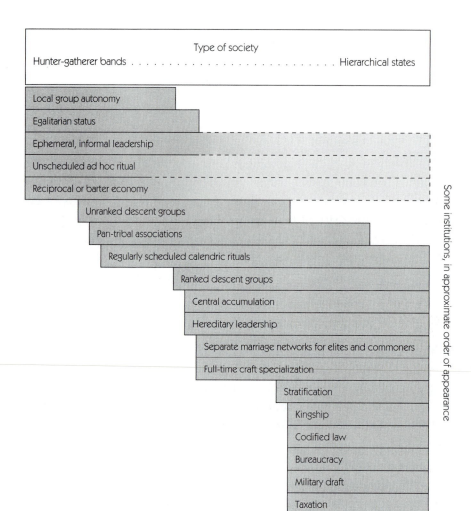

Type of society

Hunter-gatherer bands . . . . Hierarchical states

Local group autonomy

Egalitarian status

Ephemeral, informal leadership

Unscheduled ad hoc ritual

Reciprocal or barter economy

Unranked descent groups

Pan-tribal associations

Regularly scheduled calendric rituals

Ranked descent groups

Central accumulation

Hereditary leadership

Separate marriage networks for elites and commoners

Full-time craft specialization

Stratification

Kingship

Codified law

Bureaucracy

Military draft

Taxation

Some institutions, in approximate order of appearance

organization and the emergence of ranked or stratified groups within society; power and decision making are in the hands of a few. Some of the changes in social, economic, and political organization from bands to states are summarized in the figure above .

Ideology

Ideology is the means by which people structure and explain their ideas about the universe, their own place in that universe, and their relationships with one another and with other things and beings around them. Ideology permeates almost everything we do. It is reflected in the clothes we wear, the food we eat, and the places in which we live. Ideology encompasses the norms, values, and beliefs held by a society.

Ideology is reflected in cosmology—explanations of the origins of the universe, of life, and of society. Roman cosmology invoked the twins Romulus and Remus, mythical beings raised by a she-wolf, as the founders of Rome. Symbols and styles are often ideological expressions.

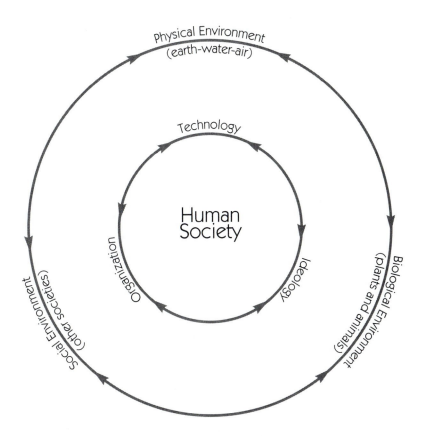

School mascots, corporate logos, flags, and certain faces incorporate and display a wide range of concepts and ideas. Ideology is often strongly expressed in ceremony and pageant surrounding important rites of passage through life: birth, adulthood, weddings, and death. Ideology is often embodied in specialists who maintain ritual knowledge and direct the ceremonies and activities that keep such ideology active and pertinent. In egalitarian societies, such individuals are known as witches and shamans—with special knowledge in ritual, healing, or seeing the future. In hierarchical societies, these roles become specialized and can be seen in the form of powerful groups such as a priesthood.

These components of human society—technology, economy, organization, and ideology—are closely interrelated in prehistoric materials. The same artifact or object may contain information on all of these aspects. A type of knife found exclusively in women's graves may hold information on the manufacture of tools, the nature of women's work, the distinction between sexes in the society, and the meaning of death. Technology, economy, organization, and ideology thus are different, but related, dimensions of past cultures and of human life and an important focus of archaeological investigations.

THE RELEVANCE OF ARCHAEOLOGY

A very reasonable question concerns the relevance of archaeology. Why should we study archaeology, why is it important to know about what happened in prehistory? One basic reason is simply to participate in the contemporary fascination with the subject. Archaeology is clearly of inherent interest to the general public. Stories appear almost daily in newspapers and on television. The World Wide Web is crowded with sites about archaeology and our human past. (A few of the more useful sites are listed in Part 5.)

But this fascination with archaeology stems from the importance of the subject. There is of course the excitement involved in unearthing treasures from the earth but, more than that, archaeology tells us about ourselves and how we got to be the way we are. Ultimately it is the lessons from our past that archaeology provides that convey its significance. The human condition is one that has changed and will continue to change over time. Archaeology tells about how humans, over millions of years, have survived and succeeded in the face of the difficult challenges of changing environments and competitive neighbors. By studying archaeology, we learn how past societies dealt with issues such as environmental change, overpopulation, political competition, success and failure.

Maybe one of the most important lessons learned in archaeology is that we are only building on what has gone on before. Archaeology allows us to see our place in the diversity of human societies and gain some appreciation for how we are alike and different. Perhaps as much as any discipline, archaeology tells us that we are all members of the family of humanity, traveling together in a miraculous journey through time.

PART 3

USING THE COMPUTER PROGRAM

The chapters in Part 3 provide a pathway through the computer program. This introduction is intended to give you some background on Fugawiland. Chapter 4, "The Menus," introduces the menus and options that are available in the program and reviews the steps to begin the project. Chapter 5, "Regional Map of Fugawiland," provides information on the topographic map and how to use it. Chapter 6, "Excavating Sites," describes how to excavate sites. Chapter 7, "Site Plans," explains how to look at the excavated sites and examine the artifacts and features that you excavated. Chapter 8, "Analysis of Data," describes the various tools in the program that you can use to study and analyze the information you have collected. Be sure to take a look at Part 4 of this book before you start the computer program; you will be filling in information from the computer in the report of investigations in that section.

FUGAWILAND

Once upon a time about two thousand years ago, several fictional groups of people lived in northern Wisconsin along the shores of Lake Superior in an area known as Fugawiland. This was an area of mild summers and very cold winters. Snow and ice would have covered the land and water during the wintertime.

These people were hunters and gatherers, unaware of the potential of domesticated sources of food, living off the wild resources of the land. Fugawiland was rich in plant and animal life. Deer, rabbits, fish, mussels, nuts, and a variety of berries, roots, and other plants provided a good diet for the people. Copper, chert, quartzite, shells, and antlers were available for making tools and other equipment.

The people of Fugawiland apparently enjoyed a very successful life-style for many years, but we know little about them other than the approximate age of the sites, the kinds of food available, and the tools they used. To better understand these settlements and the people who lived there, new excavations are essential. There are many things we would like to know.

Sites

A number of the sites from this time period have been identified from artifacts found on the surface of the ground. A map of Fugawiland with the location of the known sites is available. Sites in Fugawiland are found along the lakeshore, on the river, in the southern hills, or on the plain between the lakeshore and the hills.

As an archaeologist, you have the time and money to excavate ten sites to learn more about how these people lived. You have to decide which sites you wish to excavate. Study the location of the sites before you begin to excavate. Think about the questions you are trying to answer in your investigations. Also remember to look at the multiple-choice questions in the program as a guide to your excavations. Some of the questions may ask about specific types of sites that you need to identify.

Excavations may reveal houses, graves, fireplaces, and artifacts that have been buried in the ground. You may then analyze the information from these sites that you have excavated to learn more about the people of Fugawiland. You can get more information on how to analyze this data from these sites when you need it.

Questions

First, you will need to establish some basic information about how these people lived. Questions about what they ate, about how long and when in the year they lived at different sites, and how many people lived there may help you better understand the Fugawi adaptation.

Some of the more detailed and specific questions that archaeologists might ask about the people and artifacts from Fugawiland are listed below. Questions such as these should guide your travels through Fugawiland.

1. How many different kinds of sites are there?
2. Were any of the sites occupied for the entire year?
3. Were sites with lots of arrowheads used in springtime?
4. Where were people usually buried?
5. Did everyone have chert knives to use?
6. Were fish eaten at the inland sites?
7. What is the average size of the sites?
8. How many different groups of people lived in the area?
9. Are there any special, ceremonial sites in the area?

10. Was copper available to everyone in Fugawiland?

11. Are river mussels and deer eaten at the same sites?

12. What do the differences in the sizes of hearths mean?

13. Where are the round houses found?

14. Why are there different kinds of houses?

One way to consider questions about the past is in terms of your own life and the places you live and visit. How many different places are important (home, church, summer cottage, school, bar, gym), and what distinguishes each? What kinds of equipment and furniture are characteristic of each? How many people gather at each place? Take these questions back in time and try to understand how these prehistoric people may have lived. Assistance in finding answers to such questions can be found in the chapters in this workbook, in the Help section in the computer program, and in your own ideas and common sense about the patterns you see in the information you collect.

Fugawiland is a hypothetical place, an imaginary situation. For example, there is no chert source in northern Wisconsin, and the sites described in this area have not been discovered. Sites are usually not completely excavated, and archaeologists rarely have the kind of detailed information that is available from Fugawiland. Nevertheless, your investigation of Fugawiland will reflect the kinds of questions that archaeologists ask and the kinds of information that can be used to answer those questions. We hope that Fugawiland will teach you a good bit about the ideas and methods of archaeology.

COMPUTER PROGRAM

Computer Program

The basic pathway for the computer program is as follows. You study the map of Fugawiland, which shows the location of twenty-five archaeological sites in northern Wisconsin. You can excavate ten of these sites. Your choice of which sites to excavate is very important. Computer "excavation" will reveal the plan of the site on the computer screen, along with the distribution of artifacts, houses, hearths, burials, and other information. Through the study of the excavated sites and their contents, patterns may emerge that provide information on prehistoric diet, settlement, season of occupation, population, land use, and group affiliation.

Goals

Your analysis and interpretation of the sites and activities in Fugawiland is the focus of this exercise. You are asked to write a summary of your excavations in Part 4, "Report of Investigations." You should include in this report some information on how you arrived at your conclusions about the prehistory of Fugawiland. This summary should discuss the differences and similarities you found among sites and what those might mean.

Test Questions

IMPORTANT: Fugawiland includes a section of ten multiple-choice questions that are part of the assignment. **You can and should look at the questions before you begin to select sites in Fugawiland.** Studying the questions before you begin may help you decide where to dig. You can answer the questions, or change your answers, at any time before you complete Fugawiland. When you are ready to answer a question, enter your answer as indicated.

When you have finished your excavations, review and double-check your answers to all ten questions. When you are ready, the computer will print out your answer sheet. This answer sheet should then be given to your instructor. **You can print the answer sheet only once,** so be sure that you are finished and confident in your answers before you print.

CHAPTER 4

THE MENUS

B y now we hope you are impatient to begin your study of Fugawiland. This part of the workbook is intended to lead you through the computer portion of the assignment. Fugawiland will take several hours for you to complete. Be sure to look at the next section, Part 4, before you start the computer program.

Several features in this workbook will help you understand and complete the project. Keywords and things to do are shown in **bold** type. Keywords are defined in the glossary at the end of the workbook. Information about maps, artifacts, food sources, site analysis, and the like is also included in the Help menu of the computer program. You should make use of this Help feature frequently to learn more about the environment of Fugawiland and the sites themselves. In addition, an analysis section in the computer program will allow you to sort through the information you have excavated or to look at graphs of various categories of information. These features are explained in more detail in the following pages.

INSTALLATION

Installation instructions for Fugawiland are found in the beginning of this workbook on page ix. Please refer to those instructions and the CD's ReadMe file to install the program on your hard disk and prepare it for use.

SIGN-ON

Fugawiland opens with a series of instructions that describe the program and a set of options in a menu bar at the top of the window. This menu bar and the options provided on the computer are described in this chapter. Details on the regional map of Fugawiland, site displays, and data analysis are given in Chapters 5 to 8.

You will need to enter your name and student number at the start of the program. You can stop at any point in the program and exit and continue at a later time. Your information will be saved on the hard drive of the computer you use. You must always use the same name and student number to continue from a saved version of Fugawiland.

TIPS

- Look at the multiple-choice questions in Fugawiland before you excavate the sites. Knowing the questions in advance may help you to formulate a strategy for selecting sites.
- Use the Help section of Fugawiland. It will provide additional information that will assist you in understanding and interpreting the information you have obtained in your excavations.
- Keep notes while excavating—look for associations, jot down ideas and reasons for excavating sites, and note impressions of the sites you excavate. This will help during the analysis and write-up portions of the project.
- Always be on the lookout for patterns in the data. Try to document those patterns and others in the analysis section of the project.
- Use the Table of Sites command to see all the data from your excavations. This command lists all the artifacts and features you have uncovered, as well as other pertinent information about the site. This is also a good place to look for similarities and differences among the sites.
- Use the Sort function to order the sites in the table according to one kind of information (variable). For example, sorting on elevation will rank the sites from lowest to highest on the landscape. It is easier to look for patterns among the sites after sorting on important variables.
- Use Histogram and Plot to look at individual variables and relationships between variables.
- Many of these commands and tools are described in more detail in subsequent chapters and should be reviewed prior to using the computer program.

MAIN MENU OPTIONS

Fugawiland is designed so that you can move through the computer program easily. You can move from any part of the assignment to any other and back again using the **menus** in Fugawiland. This part of the workbook follows the arrangement of the Fugawiland menus so that you can use the two together.

The main menu bar is shown below, and the menus under each heading are shown in the margins where they are described.

```
File Regional Map Site Display Analysis Questions Window Help
```

File   Two commands are available under File in the menu bar.

Set Up Printer allows you to select the printer that will be used to print your answers, maps, and other information from the program. You can print any window in Fugawiland, including maps, graphs, plots, and site displays.

Exit allows you to leave the program. You can stop at any point and return to the assignment at a later time. The important thing is to be sure to enter your name and student number exactly the same way each time. This will enable you to return to the program where you left it.

File
Set Up Printer
Exit

Regional Map   The commands under Regional Map are used to display the map of Fugawiland and to highlight the features of the landscape and the archaeological sites. Under this heading, you will also find commands to display and excavate sites, get help, and print.

Draw Map displays a topographic map of Fugawiland with the location of twenty-five known sites in the area. The map also shows the Lake Superior shoreline, two major rivers (the Brule and the Iron), the southern hills, and the sources of copper and chert. The two major rivers are the Brule to the west and the Iron to the east. Be sure to note the north arrow and scale of the map in the northwest corner. This is a scrolling window. You can use the cursor to click in the margins of the window to scroll the map up or down, right or left. Such scrolling windows are common in Fugawiland.

Add Hills will outline the higher elevations in southern Fugawiland.

Add Rivers will mark the major river systems in Fugawiland.

Add Lake will highlight the waters of Lake Superior.

Add Sites will locate the 25 archaeological sites in Fugawiland.

Add Sources will show the sources of copper and chert in southern Fugawiland.

Display a Site produces a scrolling list of the letters of the sites you have excavated. You select one of the sites to view the excavation plans. The same command is also found on the menu bar and described in more detail below.

Excavate a Site allows you to select and excavate ten sites in Fugawiland. There are two ways to select the sites to be excavated: (1) double-clicking on the site letter on the regional map or (2) using the Excavate a Site command. The Excavate a Site command will produce a scrolling

Regional Map
Draw Map
Add Hills
Add Lake
Add Rivers
Add Shoreline
Add Sites
Display a Site
Excavate a Site
Help
Print

list of the site letter, and you can select the one you want to excavate. Sites that have already been excavated will appear in a different color on the map.

When you excavate a site, the outlines of the excavation unit will appear on your screen. To see the artifacts and features on this outline, use the right mouse button to click on the plan. This will bring up a Site Display Option box. Selecting different options in this box will allow you to see the artifacts and features at the site.

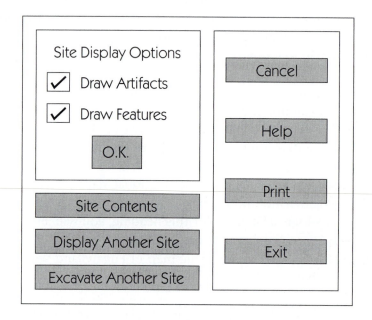

Select *Draw Artifacts* and *Draw Features* by clicking in the appropriate boxes. Clicking on O.K. will show the artifacts and features on the site plan. The artifacts will appear on the map as small dots showing the distribution of a variety of materials such as stone tools, pottery, bones, and shells. Note the concentrations of artifacts as well as areas with little material. The site display will also show all the different types of features found at the site such as houses, graves, and fireplaces. The kind and number of these features are important characteristics of the sites in Fugawiland.

Selecting the *Site Contents* box will show a table containing the counts of the various artifacts and features that were found at the site. Look for significant differences in the contents among the sites you excavate.

Clicking on *Select Another Site* will allow you to display another excavated site.

Four other options are also displayed in the Site Display Option box. *Cancel* closes the Site Display Option box without action. *Help* takes you to the Help section described below and is just another way to get

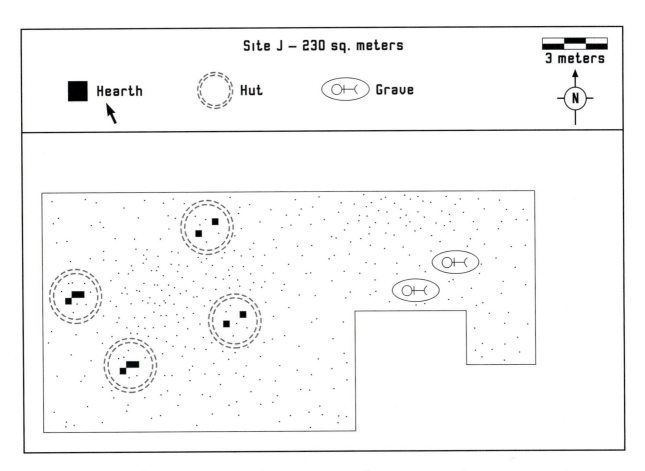

Site J – 230 sq. meters

3 meters

■ Hearth   Hut   ⊶ Grave

N

there. *Print* prints the current site information. *Exit* allows you to quit the program and return at another time.

Site Display   The command under Site Display is used to show the contents and plans of the excavated sites in Fugawiland.

> | Site Display |
> |---|
> | Select Site ... |

Select Site brings up a scrolling list of excavated sites to investigate. Selecting a site's letter designation takes you to a plan of the excavation unit at the site. Each plan is a bird's-eye view of the area that was excavated and the evidence that was found. In most cases, the excavations uncovered all of the prehistoric site. The scale of the map is the same for all of the sites, so you can compare the size and distribution of materials immediately. Again, you can click on the right mouse button to bring up the Site Display Options box described earlier.

Analysis   This is an important part of Fugawiland where you can investigate and analyze the information from the sites you have excavated. Think of this section of Fugawiland as a series of tools to use in studying the data you have obtained. These tools can be used to sort out similarities and differences among the sites and to create tables and graphs that will help you visualize these patterns. These tools are described in more detail in Chapter 8.

> | Analysis |
> |---|
> | Table of Sites |
> | Show Table |
> | Show Sorted Table |
> | Histogram |
> | Plot |
> | Regional Plot |

Table of Sites contains two commands in a submenu.

Show Table displays a large table of all of the information that you have obtained in your excavations in Fugawiland, including the site name, location, artifacts and features, and animal remains. This information is described in more detail in Chapter 7.
Show Sorted Table displays a list of all the kinds of information (variables) from the sites in Fugawiland. You can select one of these variables to use in sorting the table. For example, if you select elevation, the table will order the excavated sites from lowest to highest in elevation. With the sort tool, you can more easily look for patterns in the data from Fugawiland.

Histogram displays a list of all of the kinds of information (variables) from the excavated sites in Fugawiland. You can select one of these variables and the computer will draw a bar graph or histogram of that variable. For example, if you select elevation, the computer will draw a graph of the number of sites at different elevations in Fugawiland. The histogram tool is another way to look for patterns in the information.
Plot enables you to look at two kinds of information together. For example, you might wish to compare the number of arrowheads at each site to the elevation of the site. The computer plots the number of arrowheads at each site on the X-axis of the graph and the elevation of the site on the Y-axis. Each dot on the graph represents one site. Look for groups of dots or lines of dots. Groups of dots indicate groups of sites; lines of dots indicate trends—that sites with more of one thing also have more (or less!) of the other item. More information on histograms and plots is given in Chapter 8.
Regional Plot provides a quick way to look for differences among the sites. This command displays a list of all the kinds of information (variables) from the excavated sites in Fugawiland. You select one of these variables and the computer will draw a graph indicating the number of this variable at each site on the regional map of Fugawiland. For example, a regional plot of the number of pieces of pottery per site would show that some sites have many pieces and some sites have none. You should look at a number of different variables using the Regional Plot command.

| Questions |
| Answer Questions |

Questions   You need to answer ten multiple-choice questions, based on your investigations in Fugawiland. These ten questions are chosen specifically for you from a larger set. Each excavator gets a different set of questions to study and answer.

Answer Questions displays a series of windows with the ten questions that you need to answer. You should look at your ten questions in

Fugawiland before you begin excavating to decide what sites to excavate. You can return to these questions at any time during the assignment to review or answer them. Once you have completed Fugawiland and are satisfied with your answers, print out your answer sheet and turn it in as part of the assignment. Again, remember that you can print the answers only once.

Window   This is a standard tool for arranging and displaying the windows in Fugawiland.

Cascade provides a staggered bank of large windows one behind the other.

Tile creates multiple small screens of the open windows sized to fit in the monitor window.

Arrange Icons reduces windows to icons that you can place on the main Windows screen for later recall. Icons can be dragged around; Arrange Icons will move them to the bottom again.

Exit provides another spot to leave the program. You can also double-click on the upper left corner of the main Fugawiland window to leave the program. Be certain to enter your name and student number in the same way when you reenter the program.

Windows Open lets you select which window you want to be active in the front of the display.

Help   Help provides a standardized Windows help system. This system contains information for you as an archaeologist. It provides details on terms that are used and different kinds of artifacts, features of the landscape, and the ways archaeologists analyze the information they collect. You will find this help feature very useful for learning more about what you find in Fugawiland.

Index lists the table of contents for the Help section.

Using Help provides some instructions for using the help system effectively. Individual parts of the program are listed here as well so that you may select the area in which you need help or more information.

About Fugawiland provides some history of the program and its creators.

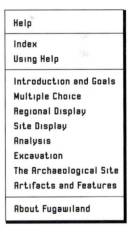

CHAPTER 5

REGIONAL MAP OF FUGAWILAND

The base map of Fugawiland (see page 72) is part of a standard topographic map of northern Wisconsin, available from the United States Geological Survey. The map shows an area that is a little more than 10,000 square kilometers, approximately 90 kilometers north-to-south and 120 kilometers east-to-west. In miles, that's about 50 by 80, the size of a large county. The major features of the landscape are shown on such maps, including lakes, rivers, and streams, roads and highways, settlements and other structures, quarry pits, and various landmarks. In addition, lines and shading on the map are used to show topographic relief, areas of forest and wetlands, and political boundaries. For example, contour lines on this map show increasing elevation from the shore of Lake Superior to the hills in the southern part of the map. Forest areas are shown in green on color maps and shaded on black-and-white ones.

Animals and Vegetation

Fugawiland lies on the southern shore of Lake Superior, where fish, mussels, and bird life may have provided important sources of food. The grass-covered plains contained few trees and likely were the home for many deer and small mammals. The rivers that run from south to north across the plains to the shore would have been important sources of both food and water.

These river and stream valleys likely were heavily wooded during the time of the Fugawi. The rolling hills in the south of the region were forested with oaks. Acorns would have been everywhere in the hills in the autumn. Deer would have been particularly numerous in these hills.

Copper

Copper occasionally is found as a natural metal in the Great Lakes region. This "native copper" can be cold-hammered into tools of various shapes and sizes. In Fugawiland, this native copper is only found in a

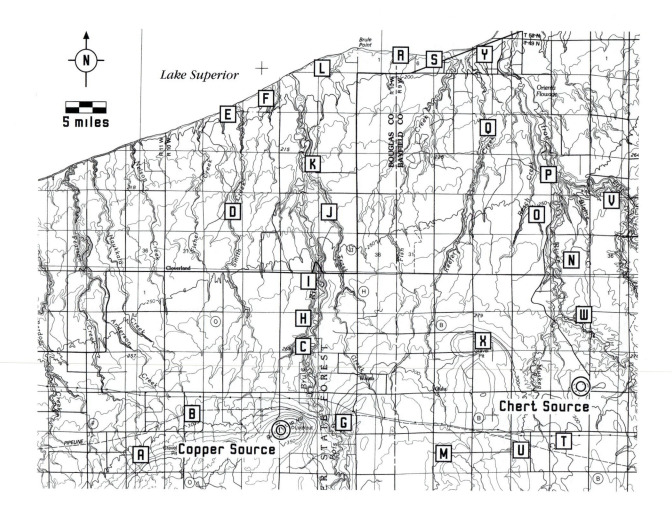

small streambed in the southwestern part of the area. We can safely assume that all the copper artifacts in Fugawiland were made of material from this source.

Chert

Chert is a fine-grained crystalline rock that was highly prized in prehistoric times because it was easy to shape by striking it with another rock or an antler hammer. Chert was used to make stone flakes with sharp edges. In Fugawiland, there is only one known source for chert, located in the hills in the southeastern part of the area. Other stone artifacts were made with quartzite, which is found everywhere.

CHAPTER 6

EXCAVATING SITES

There are two ways to select the ten sites to excavate from the twenty-five candidates in Fugawiland. You can use either one. One is simply **intuitive,** deciding which combination of sites will best represent the area. Once again, remember to look at the multiple-choice questions in the program before making your site selections. You may, for example, want to select sites in different parts of Fugawiland in order to get as many different kinds of sites as possible. You may also want to determine if there are different kinds of sites in different areas of Fugawiland. **If you want to intuitively select which sites to excavate, circle your choices on the map in Part 4 of this workbook and check the box indicating intuitive selection. You can then go to the computer program and click on the sites you have selected.**

Intuitive Sampling

A second way to select sites is to use **random sampling.** With this simple procedure, the ten sites to be excavated are selected at random rather than intuitively. Statisticians suggest using tables of random numbers to remove bias in the selection process. This method should ensure that the selected sites are well distributed on the map. Such a table appears at right. Simply close your eyes and put your finger in the table to find a starting point. From there, circle ten consecutive pairs of numbers in the table. If any of the numbers are duplicates, continue circling pairs until you have ten different numbers.

Random Sampling

Random Numbers
20 15 01 24 08 23 02 04 10 08
18 10 21 13 14 16 03 23 05 10
03 22 11 14 05 17 01 16 17 19
08 24 12 21 05 13 11 08 19 22
12 11 01 23 04 13 04 11 25 01
08 15 07 09 25 20 24 07 06 20
10 03 07 06 17 14 23 01 04 06
21 09 24 10 09 18 23 08 25 22
21 15 25 19 16 11 12 25 18 02
07 18 12 07 05 17 19 22 03 16
09 22 20 06 05 24 20 17 02 15

Next, use the table of random numbers and corresponding site letters to determine the appropriate sites for the numbers you have selected. These are the sites you should excavate.

Circle the sites you have chosen on the map in Part 4 to keep a record of your selections. At the bottom of the map, indicate that you used random numbers to select sites for excavation.

Excavation

There are two ways to excavate the ten sites in Fugawiland. **Either use the Excavate command under Regional Map on the menu bar or double-click on the letter of the site you wish to excavate on the map.** The computer will excavate each site you select and report back to you on what was found. You can excavate a total of ten sites in Fugawiland. Sites that have already been excavated are indicated and cannot be excavated a second time. As in the real world, archaeological sites are destroyed by excavation.

Think about the information you obtain in your excavations. You should consider the kinds and amounts of artifacts and features present at each site, as well as what items are absent. The next two chapters, "Site Plans" and "Analysis of Data," will allow you to revisit and reexamine the excavated sites and their contents anytime you wish.

Circle the ten random numbers and corresponding sites that you have selected.

01	A	14	N
02	B	15	O
03	C	16	P
04	D	17	Q
05	E	18	R
06	F	19	S
07	G	20	T
08	H	21	U
09	I	22	V
10	J	23	W
11	K	24	X
12	L	25	Y
13	M		

CHAPTER 7

SITE PLANS

The Site Display menu allows you to examine the contents and excavation maps of the site you selected. The first command, *Site Contents*, provides a window showing all of the different kinds of artifacts and features found during the excavation and the number of each. (This information also appears in the Table of Sites.) The artifacts and features are illustrated in the contents window, and it is important to note differences such as the kind of houses (heavy or light construction), the type of pottery (decorated with bands or zigzags) and knives (copper or chert), the size of hearths (large or small), the kind of burials (extended or bundled), and the kinds of animal bones. These categories of artifacts and features are described in more detail in below.

Next, you are given the option to display the artifacts and/or features in the excavation using the command *Site Plan*. The first thing you see in this section is an outline of the excavation area for the site. The boundaries of the excavations are indicated by the solid lines around the site. In most cases, the excavations uncovered the entire site.

Add Artifacts causes the artifacts to appear on the map as small dots showing the distribution of stone tools, pottery, bones, and shells. You should note if some areas or sites have heavier concentrations of artifacts than others. The scale of the map is the same for all the sites, so you can directly compare the size and distribution of materials in the excavations.

Add Features displays the different types of features found at the site, such as houses, graves, and fireplaces, and their location. In addition, the kinds of features present are indicated in the legend for the site plan. For example, large hearths are distinguished from small hearths, heavy houses from light houses, round houses from square houses, and extended burials from bundle burials. The kind and number of features

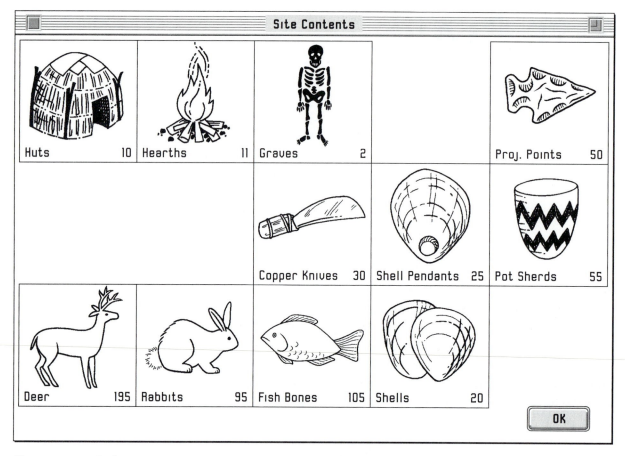

Site contents window.

at each site is important information. This information also appears in the Table of Sites.

Part 4 of this workbook contains a table for you to fill in as you excavate. **In the spaces provided, write the site designation, elevation, size, and contents to keep a personal record of your investigations.** There is also a space for notes about each site so you can record any special aspects of the site that you see. You can also print out the Table of Sites from the computer for this catalog of information.

In addition to the map and site plans, there is another important source of information about the sites you have excavated. The Table of Sites contains a summary of all information from the sites you have excavated. This table is also used in the Analysis section. These site characteristics and contents are described below in the order they appear in the Table of Site contents. Certain materials may tell you about the time of year the site was occupied or the types of activities taking place. Other objects or structures may reflect the gender of the individuals using them or perhaps the number of people present. There is a lot of information in this table.

SITE CHARACTERISTICS

Site Designation   This is simply the letter used to distinguish each of the twenty-five sites, from A to Y. These are the letters you used to select your ten sites.

Setting   This term refers to the location of the site in the landscape, whether coastal, riverine, hills, or plain. Abbreviations are used for these features. High = hills, Shor = shoreline, Riv = river, and Pln = plain.

Coordinates   These values indicate the distances north and west where the sites occur on a standard grid for the area. Higher values indicate that a site is more to the north and/or west.

Elevation   This is the altitude of a site above sea level. The greater the elevation, the higher the site in Fugawiland. Elevations are generally higher in Fugawiland as you move from north to south, from the shore of Lake Superior to the hills in the southern part of the region.

Site Size   This is a measure of the size of the site based on the spread of artifacts and features. The value is in square meters.

SITE CONTENTS

Sites are defined by the presence of features and artifacts that are the preserved remains of past human activities. These items provide important information about how and when sites were used. A great deal can be learned about prehistoric societies from the size of their sites, the kinds of activities that took place there, and the season of the year and amount of time that people spent there.

FEATURES

Features are the nonportable facilities and equipment that are products of human activity. Features include fireplaces (hearths), huts, and burial mounds. These remains often leave visible traces in the ground as an indication of structures that were created in the past.

Huts   Several kinds of structures were present in Fugawiland. Dwellings are found at some of the sites. These houses had a framework of poles and branches that supported coverings of reed mats, birchbark, or animal skins. There were both round and square huts. Both kinds of structures were about the size of an average room in a modern house. Some huts were much sturdier than others with thicker walls and more substantial construction. The type found at the site you excavate is indicated on the plan of the site.

The huts in Fugawiland likely housed four to six people. These structures often contained one or more hearths and sleeping areas for the inhabitants. One way to estimate the number of people living at a site is simply to multiply the number of houses by five.

Hearths Fireplaces are found at almost all sites in Fugawiland. They were used for cooking, heating, as a light source, and as a focal point for ceremonies. Fireplaces usually were made in a pit and show up in excavations as depressions filled with pieces of charcoal and ash. Several different sizes of hearths are present at sites in Fugawiland. The location of the fireplaces with regard to the structures may also be important. For example, more fireplaces may have been built inside houses during the winter.

Graves Burials in Fugawiland were generally simple, with a single individual placed in a shallow grave or pit. Two types of burials have been found: (1) an **extended burial,** a complete skeleton laid out in a grave, and (2) a **bundle burial,** containing only the larger bones and skull of an individual piled together in a small, circular burial pit.

These two types of burials may reflect the time of year a person died. The ground was frozen for much of the winter in Fugawiland. People who died during the colder months of the year may have been placed on outdoor scaffolds so that the flesh on the body disappeared until only the skeleton remained. Later, these bones were collected and placed in a hide bag for burial. Individuals who died during warmer months may have been buried immediately in shallow graves. A few items of food, jewelry, pottery, or other artifacts often were placed in burials as offerings and grave goods for a life after death.

ARTIFACTS

Artifacts are portable tools and materials made or modified by human activity. Artifacts include weapons and equipment as well as manufacturing refuse. These materials are often found broken at prehistoric sites as a result of being discarded or abandoned. Large quantities of such refuse at a site is the result of more people living at the place, or long periods of occupation, or both.

Projectile Points Arrows were used for hunting and perhaps as weapons in Fugawiland. The points of these projectiles were arrowheads. These points were made by "knapping," or chipping, quartzite into a desired shape. Arrowheads are usually small, one or two inches in length, with the rear end attached to a wooden shaft. These artifacts were likely associated with male activities and used for hunting deer and other animals. Sites that contain lots of projectile points may represent places where such equipment was manufactured and repaired.

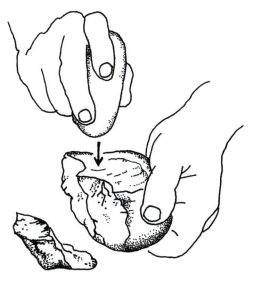

Arrowheads

Chert Knives Chert is a fine-grained stone and in Fugawiland is found only in the southwestern corner of the region. The people of Fugawiland made long, sharp knives from this chert. Chert knives with wooden or antler handles were about the size of a large kitchen paring knife, fragile but very sharp. All other kinds of stone tools in Fugawiland were made from a local quartzite that was present everywhere.

Knives

Copper Knives These sharp blades were made from native copper nuggets. The only source of copper in Fugawiland was in the southeastern corner of the region. Nuggets were shaped and flattened by hammering and then sharpened into good cutting tools, with a curved blade set in a wooden handle. The knives were roughly the size of a small hunting knife. Copper knives were durable but dulled easily. Copper was a highly valued material that may have been traded or exchanged by the inhabitants of the region.

Fishhooks These items were carved out of bone. Most of the fishhooks in Fugawiland were of medium size, perhaps two inches in length, and were used for line fishing in rivers and streams. These hooks were effective for catching bass, pike, trout, and other species. Large nets were also

Fishing

used for fishing in Fugawiland, primarily around the river mouths. Large trout are found close to shore and in the rivers around the Great Lakes primarily in the spring and summer. Fish bones show up in large quantity at some of the sites in Fugawiland.

Pendants

Shell Pendants   Shells from freshwater mussels were used to make small beads, pendants, and necklaces found at many sites in Fugawiland. First, small irregular pieces were cut out from the shell. Then holes were made in each piece using a bow drill, which uses a bowstring wrapped around a drill shaft to turn the shaft. Circular beads were made by rubbing a string of the irregular pieces on a grinding stone until they were round. Shell pendants are found only in the burials of women and children.

Pottery

Pottery   The people of Fugawiland used fairly simple pottery made from deposits of clay readily available throughout the region. Pots were made in only one form, known as jars, and were probably used for both cooking and storage. These jars were fairly large, holding about a gallon. Broken fragments of pottery vessels, known as **potsherds,** are found on all the sites in Fugawiland where cooking and/or storage activities took place.

These jars were decorated by drawing lines in the soft clay of the vessel before it was hardened in a fire. Two different styles of decoration have been identified in Fugawiland: a zigzag design (called "ZZ") and a pattern with horizontal bands (called "banded"). The location of the sites where these two different styles are found may be of use in distinguishing different groups of people in Fugawiland.

FOOD

Although the people of Fugawiland ate a variety of plants and animals, a few species provided most of the diet. These included white-tailed deer, cottontail rabbits, fish, mussels, and acorns. These species were available at different times of the year depending on climate, elevation, and other factors. It is important to consider each of these food sources in terms of where it could be found and when during the year it was available.

White-Tailed Deer This large herbivore was a major source of food for prehistoric people in the eastern United States and was abundant throughout Fugawiland. In addition to eating the meat from these animals, people used the antlers and hides as raw materials for making tools and clothing.

Deer

White-tailed deer are most easily hunted during the fall mating season when they are more curious and mobile than at other times of the year. These animals concentrate in inland areas at higher elevations during the fall and winter. The deer were hunted largely by men. Deer remains on archaeological sites are most commonly found as pieces and fragments of bones, teeth, and antlers.

Cottontail Rabbits Rabbits were another important source of food in Fugawiland, and everyone shared in snaring or trapping them. Rabbits are available year-round but are fattest in the summer, fall, and early winter. The meat is so lean in the springtime that a diet of only rabbit can lead to starvation. More energy is needed to obtain, consume, and digest the meat than it provides. Rabbits were a source of both food and fur. The skins were used to make warm blankets. The evidence for rabbits in Fugawiland is usually found as bone fragments.

Rabbits

Trout Although many species of fish were present in the waters of Fugawiland, trout provided the bulk of fish in the diet. Trout were taken with both nets and hook and line. Trout are found close to shore and in the river mouths around the Great Lakes, primarily in the spring and summer. These fish swim upstream in the fall and winter. Fish bones are often found on archaeological sites near water in Fugawiland.

Fish

Mussels Freshwater mussels flourished in the streams and along the lakeshore in Fugawiland. These shellfish contain protein but must be collected in large numbers to provide much food. Freshwater mussels are most accessible and nutritious in the fall and spring. The shells were used for beads and pendants. Shell fragments are often preserved on sites where mussels were eaten or where shell was made into finished

Mussels

artifacts. Large dumps of shells are known as shell **middens.** In areas such as Kentucky, Japan, or Denmark these middens may be 100 meters long and several meters high.

Acorns

Acorns Acorns fall from mighty oaks that grow largely in the southern portion of Fugawiland. These nuts ripen in the fall and must be collected before deer, squirrels, and other animals eat them. Acorns can be stored up to six months for the winter lean period. Acorn nutmeat was boiled, roasted, and pounded into flour in wooden mortars. Middens, or dumps, of burned acorn shells are sometimes found at sites in Fugawiland.

SUBSISTENCE PATTERNS

The combination of different foods and places used by the people of an area is described as a **subsistence pattern.** Hunter-gatherers often lived in small groups that moved from place to place during the year to take advantage of concentrations of certain food resources and to ob-

A hypothetical example of an annual cycle.

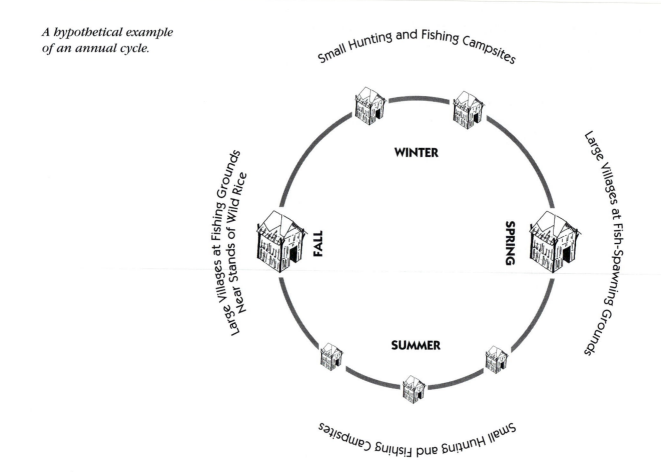

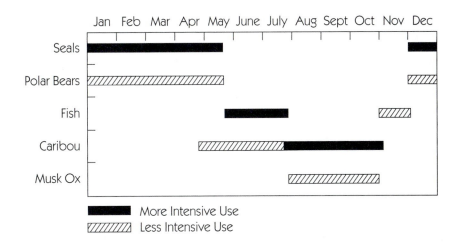

Seasonal food use among the aboriginal Copper Eskimo.

tain other needed materials. The yearly repetition of this subsistence pattern is known as an **annual cycle.** Shown above is a model of the kind of seasonal food use seen among preagricultural peoples. This example comes from the Copper Eskimo of northern Canada, where seals, polar bears, fish, caribou, and musk ox are the major sources of food at different times of the year. The different sources of food complement each other in succeeding seasons. In the case of the Copper Eskimo, seals are the important winter and spring food and are replaced by fish and caribou in the summer and fall. In the case of Fugawiland, you will need to determine the subsistence pattern from the information you collect in your investigations.

CHAPTER 8

ANALYSIS OF DATA

Are there different kinds of sites in Fugawiland? Are there seasonal or subsistence differences seen at the sites? Can these differences be seen in the size or elevation of sites or in the kinds of artifacts and features that are present? You may already have noticed some differences while you were excavating and looking at the sites. If you can distinguish several kinds of sites, you will also need to determine which sites belong to which type. Recognizing different types of sites is the best way to understand some of the patterns in Fugawiland.

TOOLS FOR ANALYSIS

There are several tools available to help you in the search for types of sites. The commands under Analysis in the menu are described here in detail. Remember also that you can look back at the site plans at any time to review the information you have obtained.

Table of Sites   Two commands are available under this menu item.

Show Table contains the basic information on the location and contents of the sites you have excavated. This is the major listing of the data for analysis. These categories of information are described in more detail below. You should look over this table very carefully to see if you can observe differences between the sites. Be sure to review the notes you made in Part 4 for ideas on the site characteristics that may reflect different kinds of sites.

Sort Table will help you study the table of information for similarities and differences. The Sort function lets you reorder the columns of information from highest to lowest values to help you look for similarities and differences among the sites. *Sort Table* first displays a list of all the site characteristics (or variables) for the excavated sites in Fugawiland. Select one site characteristic and Sort Table will order all the values for that characteristic from fewer to more, or from smaller to larger. Using the Sort option lets you look for patterns in the table more easily. With this command you can, for example, arrange all the large sites at one end of the list and the small sites at the other. The Sort command can be used with any of the site characteristics. After you have sorted one characteristic, look at the others in the table to see if they follow the same, or a different, pattern.

For example, you could ask, "Do sites at lower elevations have more arrowheads?" In the first three columns in the table below are some hypothetical numbers for site designation, site elevation, and number of arrowheads. The sites are listed in the order they were excavated. By just looking at the numbers in this table it is difficult to determine if there is any relationship between elevation and the number of arrowheads present.

Site	Elevation	#Arrowheads
Y	5	7
M	200	55
N	100	29
Q	40	15
C	130	35
X	90	33
U	210	51

Now reorder the table using the Sort Table command. Sorting on the values for elevation and then examining the values for elevation and the number of arrowheads per site will help answer this question. As you can see, the number of arrowheads does increase along with elevation.

Site	Elevation	#Arrowheads
Y	5	7
Q	40	15
X	90	33
N	100	29
C	130	35
M	200	55
U	210	51

So, the answer to the question "Do sites at lower elevations have more arrowheads?" is no. In fact, the opposite is true: Sites at higher elevations have more arrowheads. Now ask yourself why higher sites have more arrowheads.

Use the Sort command to reorder the table using other site characteristics. The Regional Plot command, described in the next section, can be used in a similar fashion to look for patterns in the site characteristics in relation to the location of sites.

GRAPHS

A graph is a visual display of information that consolidates large amounts of information, usually numbers, into a form that is easier to comprehend. Graphs provide a way to see relationships in the information you have collected. There are three kinds of graphs in the Analysis menu—Histogram, Plot, and Regional Plot—that will help you look for patterns in Fugawiland. You should use these different types of graphs to study your excavation data. The graphs may reveal similarities and differences between the sites that you had not noticed. Graphs can also tell us about relationships between different categories of data and different kinds of sites.

Histogram A histogram can be used to show how many features or artifacts you have excavated at each site. You can draw a histogram of one site characteristic at all the excavated sites.

For example, you might want to see the number of houses at each site. One way to organize this information is in the form of a table. You could tally how many houses are at each site in Fugawiland as shown in the accompanying table. In this example, there are three sites with no houses, two sites with one house, and five sites with four houses. The tally marks provide a visual summary of this information. A histogram is just a graphic version of this table of tally marks. Turn the table on its side and use the length of the bar to indicate the number of tally marks.

The Histogram command will display a graph that shows the number of houses on the X-axis and the number of sites on the Y-axis. A hypothetical graph is shown here. The location of the vertical bar indicates the number of houses per site, and the height of the bar indicates how many sites with that number of houses are present in Fugawiland.

It is also important to look for what is missing in the graph, for gaps between bars, or for significant differences in the lengths of the bars. It appears from this graph that there are some sites with no houses and some sites with more houses. Why are there no sites

# Houses	# Sites
0	III
1	II
2	
3	
4	IIIII

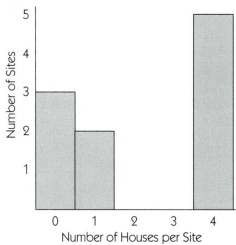

with two or three houses? Are sites without houses different from sites with houses in other ways as well?

Plot A plot is another kind of graph that allows you to look at two characteristics simultaneously. In a plot, each characteristic is plotted on its own axis. For example, in Fugawiland, we could plot the number of houses and the elevation for each site on each axis of the graph. Each dot on the graph would represent one site. Interpreting what the pattern in the dots means requires some thought. In the example plot shown here, you can see that sites with lots of houses are lower in elevation than other sites. Sites without houses are generally found at higher elevations. Study the site contents to help determine why these differences may be present.

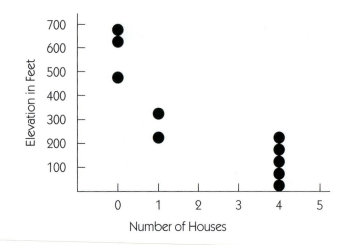

Another way to think about these plots is to use a contemporary situation. Let's say you were trying to see how different kinds of people in your class performed on exams. You might think that well-prepared students do better on exams. If you could count the number of pencils each student took to an exam (as a measure of preparedness for the exam) and compare it with exam scores, the table of information might look something like the one below. Just from looking at the table, it is hard to see if there is any relationship between pencils and scores.

Name	Number of Pencils	Hours of Study	Exam Score
Dave	5	10	90
Doug	6	7.5	85
Sally	2	3	58
Jennifer	4	14	95
Ralph	2	4	65
George	3	5	68
Vance	3	6	83
Spark	1	4	50
Carl	4	8	86
Boris	5	9	88
Lisa	2	6	74
Beth	6	11	92

If you then plotted the number of pencils against exam scores with each dot representing one student, the plot would look like this:

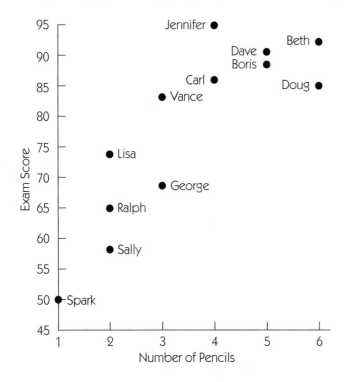

Now you can see that there is a clear trend in the linear arrangement of the dots, indicating that the more pencils one brings (that is, the more prepared one is), the better the score on the exam. You might also notice that there seem to be two groups of people in the graph. People with more pencils and higher scores appear in the upper right of the plot.

Now, pencils are probably not a very good measure of preparedness. Suppose you asked each student how many hours he or she spent studying for the exam and recorded that information. You could then draw a new plot of exam scores and hours of study, as shown on the following page. With a better measure of preparedness (hours of study), the pattern is much clearer. There is a distinct relationship between amount of time spent studying and scores on exams.

There are three kinds of patterns to look for in such plots: random, linear, and clustered. A random pattern means there is no relationship indicated in the plot.

A linear pattern means that a clear relationship is present. This is known as a **correlation;** the two characteristics are changing together. A positive trend in the line, from lower left to upper right, means that as one item increases, so does the other; a negative trend, from upper left to lower right, indicates that as one characteristic increases, the other

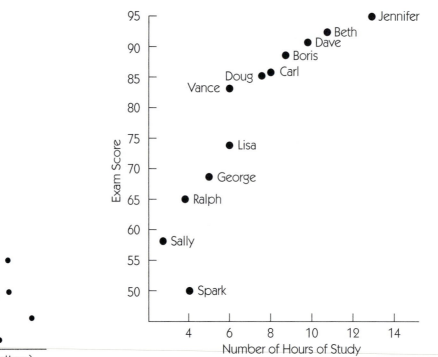

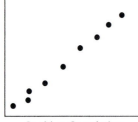

Random (no pattern)

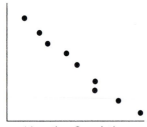

Positive Correlation

Negative Correlation

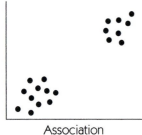

Association

decreases. For example, in the plot above, as the number of hours of study increases, so does the exam score. This is a positive correlation. If this were a negative correlation, exam scores would decrease with the number of hours of study.

A **clustered** pattern with distinct groups of dots in the plot indicates **association,** which simply means that two characteristics are found together. In the example above, there seem to be one group of dots representing those individuals with exam scores above 75 and a second group representing those with scores below 75. The two groups might be characterized as well-prepared and under-prepared for the exam. The fact that there are not middle scores on the exam suggests that long hours of study really paid off.

Now let's think about this in terms of the past. What can a plot of information about the contents of archaeological sites tell us about a prehistoric society? For example, how can the numbers of copper or chert knives at a site tell us anything? To answer, let's look at an imaginary plot of copper and chert knives by site (each dot is a site).

The hypothetical plot on the following page shows chert knives on the X-axis and copper knives on the Y-axis; each dot represents one site. Look for groups of dots or lines of dots. Groups of dots indicate groups of sites; lines of dots indicate trends—that sites with more of one thing also have more (or less) of the other item.

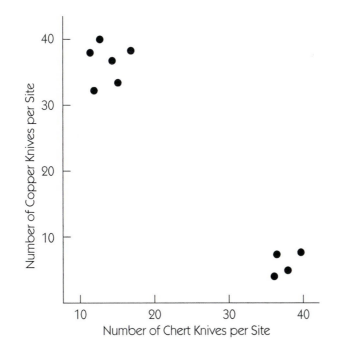

In this case, there is a clear relationship between the number of chert knives and the number of copper knives at the sites in Fugawiland. Where copper knives are common, chert knives are rare, and where chert knives are common, copper knives are rare. This is a negative correlation, and you could imagine a line running from the group on the upper left down to the group on the lower right. Two groups of sites appear in the plot: one group in the upper left with more than 30 copper knives and fewer than ten chert knives, and a second group of sites in the lower right with more than 30 chert knives and fewer than 10 copper knives. This plot indicates that the two characteristics, copper and chert knives, are not associated, not usually found together at the sites in Fugawiland. From this plot, we learn about a new pattern in the distribution of artifacts at sites in Fugawiland, and we have to ask another question, "Why are these differences present?" The answer may help you understand how people lived in Fugawiland.

Look for such relationships in your excavation data. You should be able to find similar trends among many of the site characteristics.

Regional Plot   This command provides a quick way to look for differences among the sites. Regional Plot first displays a list of all the categories of information (variables) from your excavated sites in Fugawiland. Select one and the computer will draw a graph on the map of Fugawiland indicating the relative amount of this variable using the bars from a histogram. For example, a regional plot of the number of acorns

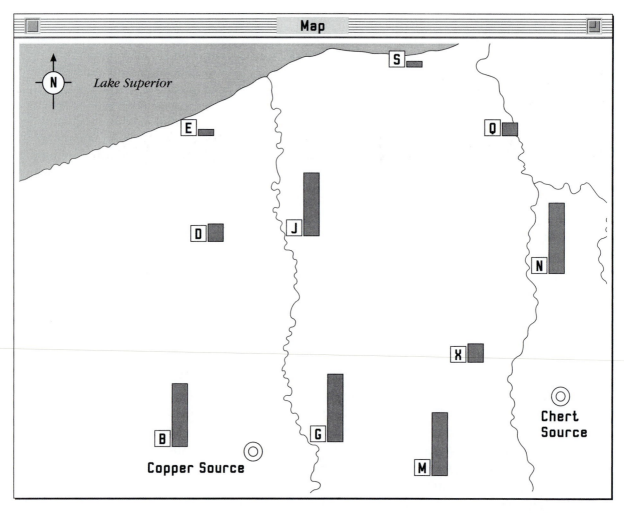

A regional plot of the number of acorns per site in Fugawiland.

per site, above, shows that some sites have many and some sites have few. The locations of sites with few and many acorns are distinct. Sites with few acorns are closer to the lake, while sites with many acorns are to the south and along the rivers. You should examine a number of different variables using the Regional Plot command. Regional plots are another way to look for patterns of association in your data, with the addition of locational information from the map.

REPORT
OF INVESTIGATIONS

INTRODUCTION

This part of the workbook is for your written report on Fugawiland. Please fill in all the information as indicated throughout as well as your name and the date above. **Note especially the areas in boldface type where specific directions and instructions are to be found.**

There are several different sections in this report. The first section deals with finding sites through interviews, field walking, artifact collection, and phosphate testing. The second section is concerned with the dating and stratigraphy of sites in Fugawiland. The third section is a summary of the results of your excavations and analyses of the information you recovered. The fourth section is a written essay on your impressions and ideas about Fugawiland and the prehistoric peoples who lived there.

When you have completed the Fugawiland project, turn in your Report of Investigations to your instructor, along with your printout of answers to the multiple-choice questions. Remember that you may want to include plans, illustrations, graphs, or other information from the computer to substantiate your findings in this report. You can print these out from the computer program as well and include them with your report. Your instructor will let you know exactly what is expected.

DISCOVERING SITES: SURVEY AND MAPPING

Bob Anderson owns a large farm in northern Wisconsin, in the area of Fugawiland. A conversation with Mr. Anderson revealed that he once found some potsherds and an arrowhead next to the river, but the items are now lost.

After some negotiations, Mr. Anderson allowed three archaeologists to survey the fields around his farmhouse. A field survey was made at 10-meter intervals. More intensive surface collections were made in areas where chipped stone artifacts, potsherds, shells, or discolorations of the soil were found. Soil samples were taken at 10-meter intervals for phosphate analysis.

The information collected during this survey is provided on the accompanying maps. These maps show the 10-meter grid that was used for the fields. Each grid square measures 10 by 10 meters. The first drawing is a sketch of the general area with some important topographic features, such as the Brule River and the Anderson farm, and the 10-meter grid on the fields.

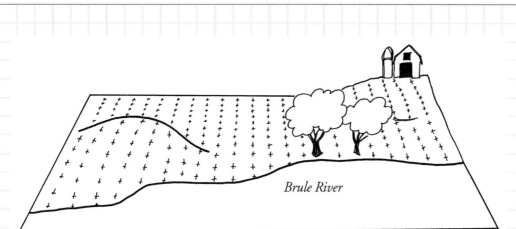

Bob Anderson's farm

The second drawing (Map 1) is the grid map of the Anderson farm with a series of numbers recorded for making a contour map. The numbers on this map are elevations in meters above sea level as measured by the surveyor. The values range from 111 to 140 meters above sea level. **Draw the contour lines on this map.** As an example, the contour line at 140 has already been drawn on the map. Add the remaining contour lines in decreasing order at 5-meter intervals—that is, at intervals of 135, 130, 125, 120, and 115 meters. This map should provide an indication of the shape of the topography on the Anderson farm and show the higher and lower areas.

Map 1: Elevation in meters above sea level.

150																			
116	115	116	115	114	115	114	115	115	115	117	121	125	129	133	137	139	140	139	140
118	117	117	116	115	117	116	116	117	116	117	120	125	129	132	136	138	139	140	139
122	123	123	122	121	122	120	117	119	119	117	121	124	129	131	132	135	139	138	138
122	127	129	129	128	129	127	126	125	123	120	120	122	126	128	130	131	130	131	132
123	127	130	131	131	131	127	127	126	125	121	120	121	125	128	129	130	130	130	130
123	127	130	131	131	131	127	127	126	125	121	120	121	124	126	128	129	129	127	127
124	128	131	132	131	132	130	129	128	128	124	120	121	124	126	128	129	129	127	127
126	128	136	136	135	134	131	132	130	129	126	122	122	122	119	120	121	122	123	124
127	130	130	139	137	137	135	136	133	129	127	124	123	120	116	116	117	118	120	121
128	130	139	140	139	139	136	138	135	131	128	124	120	118	114	115	114	115	117	117
129	133	137	141	140	140	139	139	135	130	126	121	117	115	113	113	112	113	114	115
127	131	135	136	140	139	135	134	132	130	124	121	117	114	113	112	111	112	113	113
124	128	130	131	135	135	131	129	127	125										
121	124	126	127	130															
116																			

Brule River

0   50   100   150   200

Map 2: Number of artifacts per grid unit.

Grid values (y-axis 0–150, x-axis 0–200):

150	00	00	00	00	00	00	00	00	00	00	00	00	00	00	00	00	00	00	00	00
	00	00	00	00	01	00	00	02	00	00	00	00	00	00	00	00	00	03	00	00
	00	00	00	00	00	00	00	00	00	00	00	00	00	00	00	00	00	00	00	01
	01	01	04	02	03	05	06	03	05	00	00	00	00	00	01	00	00	00	00	00
100	06	05	10	15	11	07	15	05	07	08	05	00	00	00	00	00	00	00	00	00
	10	11	22	25	20	31	25	17	11	06	09	00	00	00	00	00	00	00	00	00
	08	32	30	36	48	40	37	32	25	12	11	05	05	00	00	00	00	00	00	00
	08	36	36	48	52	52	42	36	36	15	27	00	00	00	00	00	00	00	00	00
	09	42	49	57	59	55	59	52	31	26	21	02	00	00	00	00	01	00	00	00
	13	43	55	68	65	60	53	48	46	31	18	04	00	00	00	00	00	00	00	00
50	22	41	56	66	69	72	55	54	42	35	18	02	00	00	00	00	00	00	00	00
	21	39	52	63	65	65	48	55	48	32	15	05	00	00	04	00	00	00	02	00
	19	31	48	61	62	55	41	44	39	22										
	10	10	38	48	50															
	09																			

Brule River

Map 2 shows the number of chipped stone pieces, potsherds, and other artifacts that were collected in each 10-meter grid unit during the survey. The values range from zero per grid unit to a maximum of 69 artifacts per grid unit. In order to better visualize what these numbers mean, it is useful to draw contour lines around the areas of high artifact density. **Draw contour lines of artifact density on the map.** Use a contour interval of 10 artifacts per grid unit so that the lines enclose areas of more than 10, 20, 30, 40, 50, and 60 artifacts per grid unit. These contour lines highlight the areas of artifact concentration and suggest where prehistoric people might have lived.

Map 3 shows levels of phosphate in the soil samples in the area in parts per million (ppm). Values range from 51 to 118 ppm across the survey area. Phosphate is found in bone, feces, urine, and other organic matters that accumulate in and around human habitation. Higher levels of phosphate are indicative of more human or animal activity. There is some residual phosphate almost everywhere on the Anderson farm because it has been used as pasture for cattle. **Draw contour lines on Map 3 to represent the concentrations of phosphate as an indicator of human activity.** Use an interval of 20 ppm so that the lines enclose areas containing more than 60, 80, and 100 ppm of phosphate in the soil.

Part 4 Report of Investigations

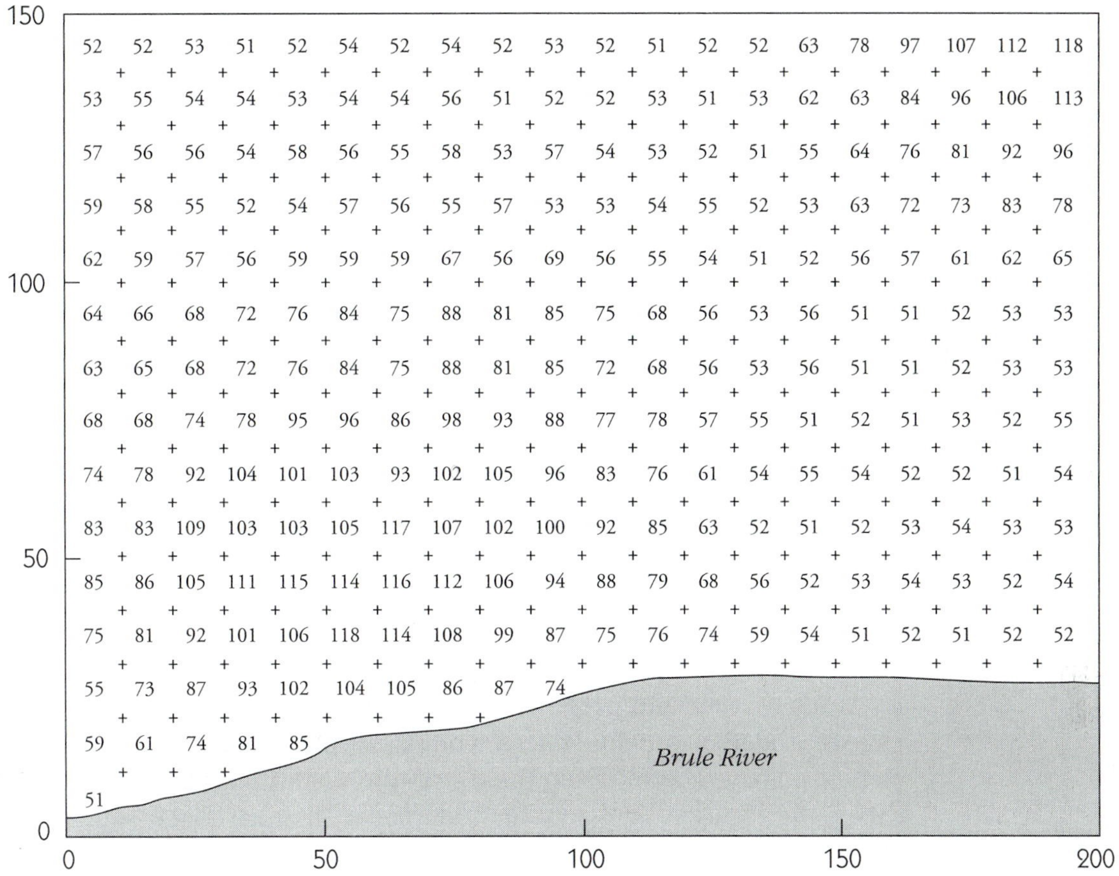

Map 3: Phosphate concentrations (ppm).

Discuss the results of the archaeological survey. What was found? What does the information from the distribution of artifacts and the phosphate values suggest? What do they tell us about the location and content of sites in this area? How many sites are in the survey area? **Answer these questions in one or two paragraphs in the space below and on the next page.**

You have time and permission to excavate four square-meter test pits in Mr. Anderson's field. Where would you place these test pits given what you have learned from the distribution of artifacts and phosphate? Mark the location of your four test pits with small black squares on Map 1, the elevation map. **Why did you place the test pits in those locations? Discuss below.**

It was surveys similar to the one done on the Anderson farm that were conducted throughout the area of Fugawiland and resulted in the discovery of the twenty-five known sites. Test pits were excavated at several of the sites in Fugawiland prior to the beginning of your excavations. These test pits were used to expose the stratigraphy of the place, to obtain samples for radiocarbon dating, and to help determine if the sites were occupied at the same time.

The stratigraphy at these sites contains both geological and archaeological layers. The cultural layer in each stratigraphic sequence represents the buried archaeological site. Analysis of the stratigraphy indicated that the archaeological layers were of approximately the same age. The stratigraphy from these sites is shown on page 100, along with the location of the radiocarbon samples that were taken. Radiocarbon sample locations are shown as black areas on the stratigraphic drawings.

Examine the strata from the various sites on the next page and work out the complete sequence for all the sites, assuming that all the individual layers occur throughout the area. You can determine the sequence of layers for the whole area by examining their order. **Fill in the chart with the appropriate symbols for the layer. Write the name of the layer beside the box that contains it. Why are some layers of different thickness at different sites? Discuss below.**

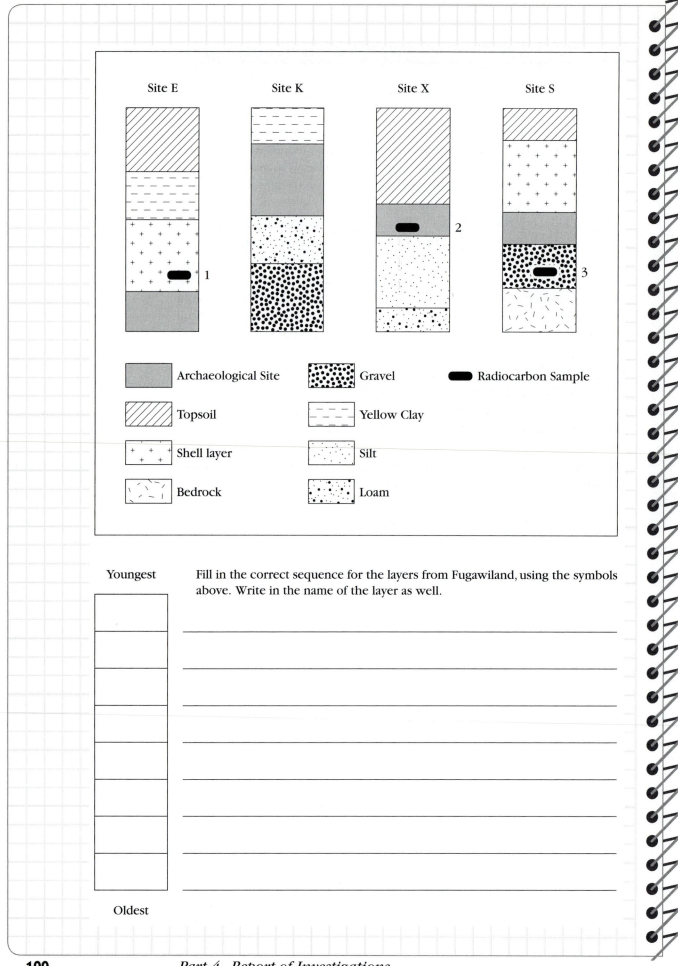

Site E   Site K   Site X   Site S

Archaeological Site   Gravel   Radiocarbon Sample

Topsoil   Yellow Clay

Shell layer   Silt

Bedrock   Loam

Youngest

Fill in the correct sequence for the layers from Fugawiland, using the symbols above. Write in the name of the layer as well.

Oldest

RADIOCARBON DATING

The charcoal samples from the test pits in Fugawiland were sent to a radiocarbon laboratory for analysis. The laboratories measured the amount of ancient carbon-14 remaining in the samples, compared to modern concentrations in the same amount of material. Measurement of remaining carbon-14 indicated the age of the samples in radiocarbon years before present (B.P.), shown in this table:

Sample	Material	Radiocarbon Years (B.P.)	Age in Calendar Years
1	Charcoal	1750 B.P.	
2	Charcoal	1860 B.P.	
3	Charcoal	2080 B.P.	

Now that you have the age in radiocarbon years B.P., you need to convert those dates to actual calendar years. Use the accompanying calibration graph. Draw a line from the bottom of the graph at the appropriate point straight up until it intersects the curvy line of radiocarbon years. From that point, draw a horizontal line to the left until it intersects the edge of the graph. The value at that point on the line represents the corrected age of the sample in calendar years. **Fill in the correct calendar years for the samples in the table above.**

Consider the information from both the radiocarbon years and the stratigraphy for the four sites in Fugawiland on the previous page. **Do these sites date from approximately the same time period? What**

evidence supports or refutes a contemporary age for the sites? Discuss below.

EXCAVATIONS

In the sections following, record the information from your excavations in Fugawiland. **First, if you have not already done so, circle the letters of the sites that you chose to excavate on the accompanying map and indicate whether you used random or intuitive sampling.**

Next, either print the Table of Sites from the computer or fill in the table on page 104 with the information from your excavations. This information is the basic data you will use in your analysis of Fugawiland. You can have the computer print out the plans of the sites, or you can sketch the most important sites that you have excavated.

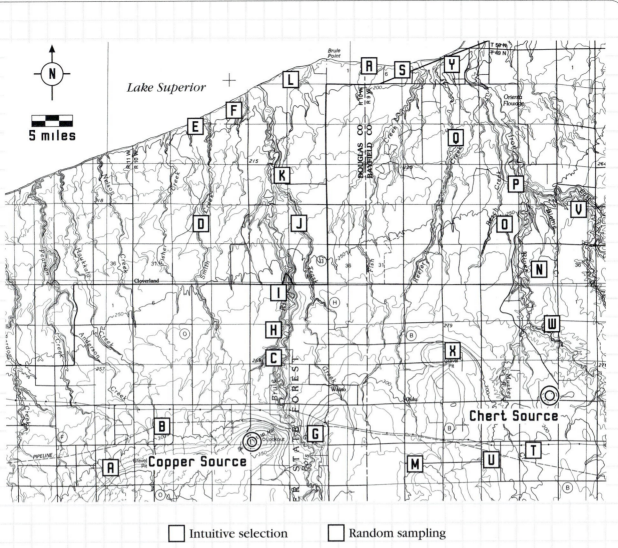

☐ Intuitive selection   ☐ Random sampling

DATA ANALYSIS

Now you have assembled all the available information from your investigations of Fugawiland. It's time to examine that information in detail to see what it can tell you about the archaeology of this area. For this part of the assignment, you should use the tools in the Analysis section of the Fugawiland program, as well as doing some calculations and drawings as indicated below.

Use the Sort and Regional Plot commands in the Analysis menu to examine different site characteristics to look for patterns, similarities, and differences. When you have sorted the different kinds of sites in Fugawiland and looked at their relationships to one other and to the landscape, you should be able to describe them in terms of their distinguishing characteristics. For example, one kind of site might contain more arrowheads and be located at higher elevations than other sites. Descriptions such as "more" and "higher" are relative to other sites. These terms are useful for distinguishing kinds of sites, but you may want to be more precise in your report. For example, you

	10	9	8	7	6	5	4	3	2	1
Site designation										
Setting										
Elevation										
Site size										
Round, heavy huts										
Round, light huts										
Square, heavy huts										
Square, light huts										
Large hearths										
Small hearths										
Extended graves										
Bundle burials										
Projectile points										
Fish hooks										
Chert knives										
Copper knives										
Shell pendants										
ZZ jars										
Banded jars										
Deer bones										
Rabbit bones										
Fish bones										
Shells										
Acorns										

Notes

might want to describe a certain type of site as being a specific number of meters in elevation.

The search for patterns in this information involves both association and correlation as described in Chapter 8. Association simply means that characteristics are found together; correlation means that certain characteristics change together. Association can be positive or negative (either things occur together or they don't). Correlation also can be positive (both characteristics increase together in amount) or negative (one characteristic increases in number while the other decreases). Association and correlation are related but different patterns. Association refers to the presence or absence of a characteristic, while correlation refers to quantities of the characteristic.

In the table below, list characteristics of the sites in Fugawiland that show association and/or correlation. Three pairs are provided as an example. Shells and lakeshore sites are found together; acorns and shellfish are negatively associated and rarely found at the same site; arrowheads and potsherds are positively correlated—that is, where there are more potsherds, there are also more arrowheads. Arrowheads and potsherds may also be negatively associated at some sites.

Fill in other pairs of characteristics that show positive association, negative association, and positive correlation in the table below based on your analysis of the data from Fugawiland.

Another way to look for differences and similarities among the sites is to calculate the average number of various artifacts, ecofacts, and other features at each kind of site. An average is calculated by taking the total number of a certain kind of artifact found in all the excavations in

Pairs of Association and Correlation in Fugawiland		
+ Association	− Association	+ Correlation
shells and lakeshore sites	acorns and shellfish	arrowheads and potsherds

Fugawiland and dividing by the number of sites. For example, if the total number of arrowheads from Fugawiland was 450 from ten sites, then the average would be 45 per site. You could then state whether a site had more or fewer than the average number of arrowheads per site.

Calculate the averages for the different categories of artifacts and other materials from Fugawiland that are listed in the table below. (Divide the total number of the item found at all the sites by 10, the total number of sites.) What do these averages tell you about the different sites in Fugawiland? **Discuss your results below.**

Average Number of Category by Site		
Category	Total Excavated	Average (Total/10)
Arrowheads		
Elevation		
Graves		
Potsherds		
Houses		
Site Size		

You can learn other useful information by calculating the density of artifacts and features at the sites in Fugawiland. Density is a measure of the number of items in a given area. You can determine the density by dividing the total number of one kind of artifact or feature from the site by the size of the site. This calculation gives you the density of materials per square meter of the excavated site. You can compare this figure among sites. For example, some sites may have a much higher density of pottery or fish bones than others. **In the accompanying table, calculate the density of potsherds and arrowheads at the ten sites you excavated in Fugawiland. Discuss your results below.**

Artifact Density by Site					
Site Letter	Site Size (m²)	Potsherds Number	Density	Arrowheads Number	Density

Another way to consider how the artifacts and other materials are distributed at sites in Fugawiland is to calculate the percentage of items at each site. For example, what percentage of all pottery is found at each site you excavated? Percentages are calculated by dividing the number of potsherds found at one site by the total number of potsherds from all the excavated sites in Fugawiland. Then multiply that number by 100.

In the next table, calculate the percentage of potsherds and points from all ten excavations that were found at each of the sites you excavated. (Fill in the number of each category at each site. Calculate the total number of points and potsherds from the excavations at Fugawiland. Divide the number from each site by this total and multiply by 100 to determine the percentages. Be sure to write in the letter designation of each site. The sum of the percentages should be 100 percent for both pottery and points.) **Look for any patterns in the percentage data. Discuss your results below.**

Artifact Percentages by Site

Site Letter	# Sherds	Sherds/Total	X100 = %	# Points	# Points/Total	X100 = %
TOTAL			100%			100%

It's a good idea to draw some histograms and plots by hand so that you understand what such charts mean and how they are made. You can review the section on histograms and plots on pages 87–92. Then you can practice creating them here. **Fill in the accompanying tables with the appropriate information from your excavations.** Then transfer the information to the graphs. The first two graphs are histograms for the number of points and the number of copper knives per site, and the last

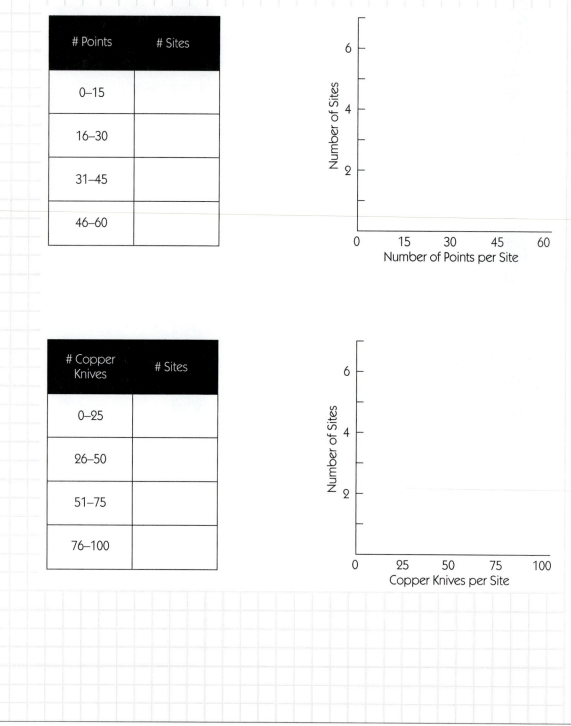

# Points	# Sites
0–15	
16–30	
31–45	
46–60	

# Copper Knives	# Sites
0–25	
26–50	
51–75	
76–100	

two are scatter plots for elevation vs. site size and elevation vs. number of pendants. **Fill in the appropriate bars and dots from the information you obtained in your investigations of Fugawiland.**

You should use the Histogram and Plot functions in the Analysis section of the Fugawiland computer program to look at many different site characteristics in your search for patterns. **Attach the most informative of these graphs to your Report of Investigations.**

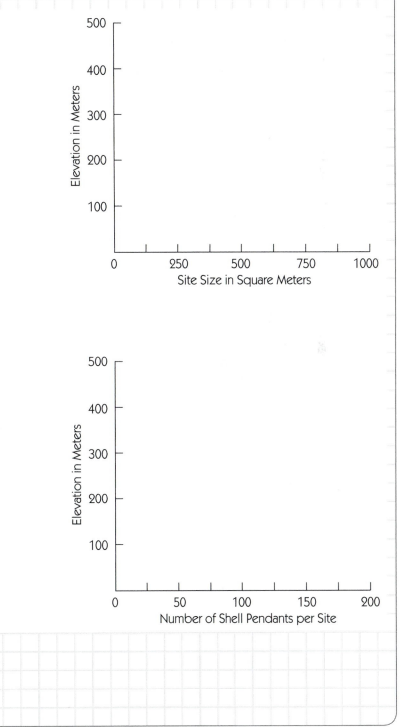

Site	Site Size	Elevation

Site	Pendants	Elevation

SEASONAL FOOD USE

The seasonal pattern of resource availability in Fugawiland is an important factor in people's lives. Given the information you learned from your excavations and what you know about Fugawiland, describe the probable annual cycle. You can review information about seasonal activities on pages 82–83.

Fill in the chart below to indicate what time of year the foods listed were used in Fugawiland. Use a solid black bar for more intensive use and diagonal lines for less intensive use. Discuss this graph and the annual subsistence pattern in Fugawiland below.

	Jan	Feb	Mar	Apr	May	June	July	Aug	Sept	Oct	Nov	Dec
White-tailed Deer												
Cottontail Rabbit												
Lake Trout												
Freshwater Mussels												
Acorns												

■ More Intensive Use
▨ Less Intensive Use

THE REPORT

As part of the Fugawiland assignment, **write a brief essay,** giving your interpretation of the prehistory of Fugawiland, and include it with your Report of Investigations.

The focus of this essay should be on the settlement and subsistence patterns that you discovered in your excavations and analysis. Your essay should **consider the following questions:**

- How many types of sites are present in Fugawiland?
- What kinds of food were eaten in Fugawiland?
- What foods were obtained, from where, and at what times of the year?
- What kinds of information were most useful for distinguishing the different types of sites?
- How many groups of people were present in Fugawiland, and how did they differ?
- What information is useful to distinguish these groups? (You might want to consider issues like group size and subsistence, or distinctive kinds of artifacts.)
- Is there evidence of trade or exchange?
- What other kinds of information would you like to have to better understand the archaeology of Fugawiland?

In addition to the written part of your essay, attach site plans, maps, and/or graphs and your computer answer sheet to document your ideas and arguments.

PART 5

FOR FURTHER STUDY

The books listed below are recommended for additional information to individuals interested in some of the subjects discussed in Fugawiland. There are a number of good books on these subjects, and we have indicated only a few. To learn more, look at these books and track down some of the additional references they list. Following a trail of references is the best way to learn more about a subject.

General Introductions to Archaeology

Ashmore, Wendy, and Robert J. Sharer. *Discovering Our Past: A Brief Introduction to Archaeology.* 3rd ed. Mountain View, CA: Mayfield, 2000.

Feder, Kenneth L. *The Past in Perspective: An Introduction to Human Prehistory.* 2nd ed. Mountain View: CA: Mayfield, 2000.

Price, T. Douglas, and Gary M. Feinman. *Images of the Past.* 3rd ed. Mountain View, CA: Mayfield, 2001.

Renfrew, Colin, and Paul Bahn. *Archaeology: Theories, Methods, and Practice.* London: Thames and Hudson, 1998.

Thomas, David Hurst. *Archaeology: Down to Earth.* New York: Harcourt Brace, 1999.

Wenke, Robert. *Patterns in Prehistory.* Oxford: Oxford University Press, 1997.

Methods of Archaeology and Fieldwork

Barker, Philip. *Techniques of Archaeological Excavation.* London: Routledge, 1993.

Drewett, Peter. *Field Archaeology. An Introduction.* London: Routledge, 1999.

Hester, Thomas R., Harry J. Shafer, and Kenneth L. Feder. *Field Methods in Archaeology.* 7th ed. Mountain View, CA: Mayfield, 1997.

McMillon, William. *The Archaeology Handbook. A Field Manual and Resource Guide.* New York: John Wiley & Sons, 1991.

Renfrew, Colin, and Paul Bahn. *Archaeology: Theories, Methods, and Practice.* London: Thames and Hudson, 1998.

Sutton, Mark Q., and Brooke S. Arkush. *Archaeological Laboratory Methods.* Dubuque, IA: Kendall/Hunt, 1998.

North American and Great Lakes Indians

Fagan, Brian. *Ancient North America: The Archaeology of a Continent.* London: Thames and Hudson, 1995.

Jennings, Jesse. *Ancient Native Americans.* San Francisco: Freeman, 1989.

Mason, Carol. *Introduction to Wisconsin Indians: Prehistory to Statehood.* Salem, WI: Sheffield, 1988.

Mason, Ronald. *Great Lakes Archaeology.* New York: Academic Press, 1981.

Quimby, George. *Indian Life in the Upper Great Lakes.* Chicago: University of Chicago Press, 1960.

Ritzenthaler, Robert, and Lynne Goldstein. *Prehistoric Indians of Wisconsin.* WI: Milwaukee Public Museum, 1985.

Computers and Data Analysis

Dibble, Harold L., Shannon P. McPherron, and Barbara J. Roth. *Virtual Dig: A Simulated Archaeological Excavation of a Middle Paleolithic Site in France.* Mountain View, CA: Mayfield, 2000.

Drennan, Richard. *Statistics for Archaeologists.* New York: Plenum/Kluwer, 1996.

Fletcher, Mike, and Gary Lock. *Digging Numbers: Elementary Statistics for Archaeologists.* Oxford: Oxford University Committee for Archaeology, 1994.

McPherron, Shannon P., and Harold L. Dibble. *Using Computers in Archaeology: A Practical Guide.* Boston: McGraw-Hill, 2002.

Richards, J. D., and N. S. Ryan. *Data Processing in Archaeology.* Cambridge: Cambridge University Press, 1985.

Shennan, Steve. *Quantifying Archaeology.* New York: Academic Press, 1988.

Thomas, David Hurst. *Refiguring Anthropology.* Ashland, OR: Waveland Press, 1993.

Fieldwork Opportunities

Many universities run field schools in the summer for undergraduate students. Departments of anthropology in most universities have a listing of these field school opportunities around the country. The journal *Archaeology* publishes a list of fieldwork opportunities each spring. Several organizations provide brief fieldwork opportunities for those who can afford them: Earthwatch (P.O. Box 403NP, Watertown, MA 02272; phone 800-776-0188); University Research Expeditions Program, University of California–Berkeley (Berkeley, CA 94720; phone 510-642-6586); Smithsonian Research Expeditions (490 L'Enfant Plaza SW, Suite 4210, Washington, DC 20560; phone 202-287-3210). Most of these organizations have Web sites where you can also find this information.

World Wide Web

There are now thousands of Web sites on archaeology on virtually every subject, area, and time period. A few major sites with links to many others are listed below as an entry into the World Wide Web of archaeology. Remember, too, you can use a search engine like www.google.com or www.yahoo.com to locate many archaeology Web sites.

The Society of American Archaeology **www.saa.org**
Archaeology on the Net **www.serve.com/archaeology**
Archaeology, journal and Web guide **www.archaeology.org**
Internet Archaeology, an electronic journal **intarch.ac.uk**
Discovering Archaeology, journals **www.discoveringarchaeology.com**
Archaeology Resources on the Net **archnet.asu.edu/archnet/default**

GLOSSARY

absolute dating: Dating that assigns a specific, calendar age. Coins and artifacts related to historical events can be absolutely dated. Radiocarbon dating also provides absolute dates.

aerial photographs: Mapping of an area through series of photos taken at elevations ranging from those of low-flying planes to satellites.

annual cycle: The changes in subsistence and settlement among hunter-gatherers, who move during the year to take advantage of the availability of food; also called *seasonal round.*

archaeology: The study of the past through material remains.

artifact: Portable object made by people in the past.

association: A relationship between two characteristics that occur together. Items found together in archaeological contexts are said to be in association. See also *correlation.*

bundle burial: Secondary burial of parts of the skeleton after the flesh and soft tissue have disappeared.

burial: Graves found individually or grouped together in distinct burial areas. Several different kinds of burials can be found. See also *inhumation, bundle burial,* and *cremation.*

calibration: Refers to the correction of radiocarbon years to calendar years by means of a curve or formula derived from the comparison of radiocarbon dates and tree rings from the Bristlecone pine tree. This calibration extends approximately 6000 years into the past.

classification: Divisions of objects into groups on the basis of shared characteristics.

contour map: Chart of the topography or shape of the landscape with curving lines used to represent changing elevation.

correlation: A relationship between two variables that change together. Correlation can be positive—both characteristics increasing or decreasing, or negative—one characteristic increasing while the other decreases.

cremation: Burial of ashes and fragments of carbonized bones from a body that has been burned prior to burial.

dating methods: Determination of the age of archaeological remains.

datum: The fixed point or center of gravity for a grid. Distances on the grid are measured from the datum point.

ecofact: Remains of plants, animals, sediments, and other materials that result from human activity.

economy: Broadly, the ways and means by which people obtain food, materials, and goods to sustain their lives.

ethnicity: Refers to differences among groups of people that may appear in language, customs, values, and other cultural behaviors.

excavation: Exposure and recording of buried materials from the past.

exchange: Aspect of the economy that involves the movement of food, goods, or materials between groups or individuals. Exchange can take place in several different ways.

extended burial: Simple inhumation of the dead in a grave.

extraction sites: Locations for specific materials or kinds of resources.

faunal analysis: Study of prehistoric animal remains.

feature: Immovable structures or layers, pits, and posts in the ground.

fieldwork: Discovery of archaeological sites in the landscape through surveys and excavations.

form: Size and basic shape of an object.

function: The presumed or known use of an artifact.

fusion: The closing of sutures between bones of the skull, or the joining of ends of limb bones to the shaft; used to determine age of death.

geophysical prospecting: Search in the subsoil for prehistoric features by measurement of magnetic variations, conductivity of the soil, or ground-penetrating radar.

georadar: Technique for subsurface survey using microwave radiation to penetrate the first few feet of the ground and record irregular features beneath the surface.

ideology: Shared ideas structuring the relationship between people and the universe, among people, and with other things and beings around them.

inhumation: Extended burial of the whole body, usually with all the bones in the right position.

intuitive sampling: Subjective choice of sample locations that appear to be most representative of the whole study area.

level: Simple field surveying instrument used to measure the elevation and distance of points in the field.

locational analysis: Examination of the geographic distribution of artifacts within a site or sites across across the landscape.

macrofossil: Visible remains of past animals, insects, fish, or plants at archaeological sites.

menu: List of options for running a computer program that appear on the screen.

midden: Trash heap or accumulation of waste; the garbage dumps of prehistoric sites. A shell midden is a specific kind of midden comprised of shells.

osteologist: A scientist trained in the study of prehistoric bone remains. These individuals often concentrate on either human or animal bones and look for information on the age and sex of skeletons, manner of death, season of death, signs of dismemberment, and the like.

phosphate analysis: Measurement of phosphate concentrations in soil as an indicator of past human activity. Phosphate is present in bone, feces, urine, and other organic matters that accumulate around human habitations.

physical anthropologist: Anthropologist who studies the physical and biological evolution of humankind.

place names: Names of towns and other landmarks that may reflect the origin of earlier settlers or the activities or resources that attracted them to the area.

pollen: Microscopic plant reproductive grains; size and shape are distinct to each species of plant.

potsherd: Broken fragment of a pottery vessel.

radiocarbon dating: Absolute dating method based on the principle of radioactive decay in carbon.

random sampling: Statistical way to take a sample through use of random numbers and without any previous bias.

relative dating: Age of the object evaluated in relation to other objects. See also *absolute dating*.

sample: A portion that is representative of the larger region under investigation.

section: Vertical wall of soil in test pits, trenches, and dissected features. "Section," or "balk," is also the term used for walls of deposits left untouched in the excavation area in order to study the stratigraphy in relation to the horizontal layers.

settlement: Habitation site.

site: Accumulation of artifacts and/or ecofacts, representing a place where people lived or carried out certain activities.

social organization: Roles and relationships among people in society.

sodality: A group or club within a society that helps to integrate members of the entire community.

stratigraphy: The sequence of layers accumulated through natural and/or human activities. The bottom layer is deposited first and is the oldest while the layers above are progressively younger—the law of superposition.

style: Color, texture, and decoration of the object according to cultural norms and individual choice.

subsistence: Resources and activities by which people feed and shelter themselves.

survey: Search of the landscape for artifacts and sites on the ground through aerial photos, field walking, soil analysis, and geophysical prospecting.

technology: Knowledge and manufacturing techniques that allow conversion of raw materials into finished products and equipment.

test pit: Small excavation units, usually only one or two meters square, intended for a preliminary examination of the contents and stratigraphy of a site.

topographic map: A map of the shape of the surface of the landscape showing elevation with contour lines, bodies of water, roads and settlement, and other landmarks.

topography: Shape and structure of the earth's surface in terms of elevation, bodies of water, and other features.

total stations: Modern surveying instruments that employ global positioning satellites, a radio survey system, and computerized display.

INDEX

geophysical prospecting, 19
georadar, 19–20
glossary, 119–122
government, 55
graphs, 87–92
graves. *See* burials

hardware requirements, ix
health, bone analysis and, 45, 46
hearths, 78
help
  menu for, 69
  resources for, ix
hierarchical societies
  ceremony and ritual in, 57
  complexity and, 53, 55–56
  rank and class in, 54
  transition from egalitarian
    society, 55–56
  See also agricultural societies
hierarchy, 55–56
  See also class
Histogram command, 87–88
histograms, 87
horizontal (area) excavations,
  32–35
household, as economic
  component, 54
hunter-gatherers
  division of labor in, 54
  as egalitarian society, 54, 55,
    56, 57
  as subsistence pattern, 53,
    82–83
  See also agricultural societies
hunting, faunal analysis and, 42,
  44
huts. *See* dwellings

ideology, 56–57
inhumations (extended burials),
  45, 78
inorganic ecofacts, 42
installation instructions, ix
intuitive sampling, 73

kinship, 53, 54

landowners, consultation with, 9
level, 13
library research, 7–8

lineages, 54
linear plot pattern, 89–90
lithic specialists, 39

macrofossils, 42
males. *See* gender roles; sex
  (biological)
maps
  contour, 11–17
  site grids, 26
  sources of, 8
  topographic, 8, 71
marriage systems, 53, 54, 57
men. *See* gender roles
menu options, 64–65
  Analysis menu, 67–68
  File menu, 65
  Help menu, 69
  Questions menu, 68–69
  Regional Map menu, 65–67
  Site Display menu, 67, 75–77
  Table of Sites menu, 76–83,
    85–87
  Window menu, 69
metal detectors, 19
methods of inquiry, 7–11
  aerial photographs, 8
  archival and library research,
    7–8
  fieldwork. *See* fieldwork
  topographic maps, 8, 71
  See also archaeology
micromorphology, 39
middens, 45, 82
mussels, 80, 81–82

Native Americans
  burial protection of, 46
  Copper Eskimo, 82–83

organic ecofacts, 42
osteology, 39, 46

paleoethnobotany, 39
pendants, shell, 80
percentage, calculation of, 108
phosphate analysis, 17–18
photographs, aerial, 8
physical anthropology, 39
plant remains, 42
pollen, 33, 42

specialists in analysis of, 39
  See also animal remains; bones
Plot command, Regional, 91–92
plots, 88–91
political organization, 55, 56
pollen, 33, 42
postholes, 32, 33, 35
potsherds, 80
pottery, 39, 80
privacy, 47
production. *See* division of labor
projectile points, 79
publication of results, 36

quartzite, 72, 79
Questions menu, 68–69

rabbits, 81
radiocarbon dating, 49–52
random plot pattern, 89
random sampling, 73
rank, 54
  See also class
reciprocal exchange, 53
recording information, 10–11
  as archival activity, 25, 36–37
  artifact catalog, 33, 40–41
  conditions of observation,
    10–11
  elevation, 11–16, 26
  field laboratory and, 23
  horizontal (area) excavation,
    33, 35
  post-dig handling of records,
    36
  site grids, 26
  See also maps
redistribution, 53
Regional Map menu, 65–67
Regional Plot command, 91–92
regional settlement patterns,
  47–48
relative dating, 29, 31, 48
research, library and archival, 7–8
resistivity meter, 19
rites of passage, 57

samples
  excavation and, 33
  surveys and, 9
sampling, 73

secondary (bundle) burials, 45, 78
sections (of excavation), 27
sediments. *See* soil; stratigraphy
settlement archaeology, 46–48
settlements, 47–48
    See also sites
sex (biological)
    of humans, skeletal analysis, 46
    of prey animals, 42
    See also gender roles
shell artifacts, 80, 81–82
sifting, 33
sign-on to program, 63–64
Site Display menu, 67, 75–77
site grids, 26
sites
    datum point for, 13, 26
    defined, 7
    destruction of, 24–25, 36
    excavation of. *See* excavations
    extraction, 48
    geophysical prospecting, 19
    grids of, 26
    phosphate analysis of, 17–18
    selection of, 24–25
    size of, 47
    soil contents, 18
    surveys of. *See* surveys
    test pits, 17, 18, 26–27
    testing of, 7, 16–18, 26–27
    See also Fugawiland;
      settlements
social organization, 53–54
    complexity and, 53, 55–56

See also economy; egalitarian
    societies; hierarchical socie-
    ties; political organization
sodality, 53
soil
    analysis of excavated, 44
    contents of, 18
    geophysical prospecting, 18–19
    phosphate analysis, 17–18
    sifting of, 33
specialists
    field director's reliance on, 23
    types of, 39, 42, 44
specialization. *See* division of
    labor
stadia rod, 13, 14
states (as society), 55–56
status, 47, 54, 55–56
stratigraphy, 28–31, 48
style
    classification of artifacts by, 41
    as ideological expression,
      56–57
subsistence patterns, 52–53,
    82–83
    See also agricultural societies;
      hunter-gatherers
surveying instruments, 13
surveys
    contour maps and, 11–17
    defined, 7
    field walking, 9–10
    permission for, 9
    samples, 8

See also excavations; fieldwork;
    sites; testing
symbols, 56–57

Table of Sites menu, 76–83, 85–87
technology
    classification of artifacts by, 41
    reconstruction of past societies
      and, 52
    See also tools
testing, 7, 16–18, 26–27
test pits, 17, 18, 26–27
tools
    classification of, 41
    gender roles and, 57, 79
    soil testing and toolmaking
      evidence, 19–20
    specialists in study of, 39
    types of, 79–80
    See also artifacts
topographic maps, 8, 71
topography, 8
total stations, 13, 26
trade, 53
transit, 13
tribes, 55, 56
trout, 81

vertical excavations, 27–31
villages. *See* settlements

Web sites on archaeology, 117
Window menu, 69
women. *See* gender roles